CEYLON
UNDER THE
BRITISH

G. C. MENDIS

GYAN

Published by

GYAN

Gyan Publishing House
5, Ansari Road
Daryaganj, New Delhi-110002
Phone: 011-47034999, 9811692060
E-mail: books@gyanbooks.com

Distribution Network
gyanbooks.com
India, USA, Canada, UK, Australia, France

ISBN : 978-81-212-3217-3 (PB)
First Published, Colombo, 1952

2nd Impression 2020

Printed at: Gyan Press, Delhi.

Ceylon
Under the British
Author: G. C. Mendis

CEYLON
UNDER THE
BRITISH

TO

L. E. BLAZE

Founder and First Principal
of Kingswood College

PREFACE TO THE FIRST EDITION

The British Period of Ceylon History was studied from works like Emerson Tennent's *Ceylon* and other original sources till there appeared in 1900 Mr. L. E. Blaze's little *History of Ceylon* which included a chronological account of the chief events under the rule of British Governors. It satisfied a demand and went to a tenth edition in 1937, being brought up-to-date with each new edition.

Twenty-six years later H. W. Codrington published his critical *A Short History of Ceylon*, but he dealt with the British administration only up to 1833. Three years earlier L. J. B. Turner published *The History of the Maritime Provinces*, 1795-1803. It covered only about eight years, but its thoroughness and comprehensiveness gave a good start to larger works.

In 1932 appeared Rev. Father S. G. Perera's *A History of Ceylon for Schools*, 1505-1911, in which about two hundred pages were allotted to the British Period. It gave a fairly comprehensive account of the main developments under British rule and is the most widely read today for a study of the British Period. In the following year Professor L. A. Mills of Canada published *Ceylon under British Rule*, 1795-1932. This scholarly work dealt in fair detail with the period up to 1889, and in outline up to 1932.

In 1939 Dr. Paul E. Pieris brought out his *Trisinhala* giving a detailed account of British relations with Kandy. This was followed by Dr. Colvin R. de Silva's work, *Ceylon under the British Occupation*, 1795-1833, which provided for the first time a really comprehensive and scientific survey of the early British Period.

Similar works dealing with the rest of the British Period are urgently needed. Till then it is hoped that this book will be of some service. It is meant not to replace but only to supplement the works that have already appeared, to all of which I wish to acknowledge my obligations. Dr. de Silva gave me permission to make use of the material in his book, and but for this act of kindness and the comprehensive view he gave of the early British Period this work might not have seen the light of day.

I am indebted for information to numerous other publications as well as contributions to magazines. Space does not permit me to refer to each one of them separately. But I have given elsewhere a list of the more important works to which the reader may go for further material.

This book was written from time to time whenever I could snatch some leisure from my teaching work at the University. It does not pretend by any means to be an exhaustive or thorough work, and it is likely that many who have studied more deeply some aspects dealt with in the book will find it wanting. To them I shall be grateful for their criticisms. And I hope the defects of this work will stir others to carry on further research.

I have to thank Professor E. F. C. Ludowyk, Mr. W. J. F. LaBrooy and Mr. E. P. Mendis who took keen interest in the work. They read through the entire manuscript and gave me valuable advice and criticism. I am also grateful to Mr. S. Dutt, Mr. J. de Lanerolle, Rev. C. N. V. Fernando and Mr. K. L. V. Mendis for their assistance.

G. C. MENDIS

PREFACE TO THE SECOND EDITION

A certain number of changes have been made in this edition. The Introduction has been re-written in greater detail. The text has been revised and the sections in certain chapters have been re-arranged.

G. C. MENDIS

1st July, 1945.

PREFACE TO THE THIRD EDITION

A considerable number of important changes have been made in the text of this edition, especially in the early chapters. In some places additions have been made and in others the subject-matter has been re-arranged. Further minor changes have been made to remove ambiguities or errors that have crept in.

I am indebted to Mr. W. J. F. La Brooy for many of the changes. He placed at my disposal many facts he had gathered through his own study of the British Period of Ceylon History besides offering valuable criticisms of the book as a whole.

G. C. MENDIS

1st November, 1951.

PRONUNCIATION OF CEYLON NAMES

ā as in f*a*ther

ä as in c*a*t

ā̈ as in *a*nt

ē as in m*e*t lengthened

ī as in f*ee*t

ō as in m*o*te

ū as in b*oo*t

CONTENTS

CHAPTER PAGE

PART III
FROM CROWN COLONY TO FULL RESPONSIBLE GOVERNMENT

LIST OF MAPS

LIST OF MAPS

CHAPTER I

INTRODUCTION

1. THE ANCIENT PERIOD

The history of Ceylon may be divided into three periods, ancient, medieval and modern, which possess definitely marked characteristics of their own. These periods do not necessarily correspond to the similar divisions in European history. The ancient period of Ceylon, for instance, has little in common with the Greek and Roman developments in Europe, and reflects mainly Indian developments under the Mauryas, the Sātavāhanas, the Guptas, the Pallavas and the Dravidian Cōlas.

The ancient period extended from about the fifth century B.C., when the speakers of an Aryan dialect settled in this island, to about the end of the twelfth century A.D., when Polonnaruva ceased to be the capital of Ceylon owing to the invasion of Māgha of Kalinga. It was the period of the greatest achievements of the Sinhalese. The four ancient cities of Anurādhapura, Māgama, Sīgiriya and Polonnaruva flourished during this time. To it also belonged the irrigation tanks, described by John Still in *The Jungle Tide* as 'the finest item of the ancient Sinhalese culture and the most beautiful feature of the country excepting only the mountain peaks and valleys'.

The civilization of this period was essentially of the Dry Zone. The south-western quarter of the island, the Wet Zone, was the least developed area at this time. The people lived in isolated villages, produced their own food and most of their other necessities, and depended little on the rest of the country. There were, however, two problems with which they could not cope. Living as they did in the Dry Zone, they obtained rain during the north-east monsoon only, and that supply was inadequate to carry on the cultivation of rice, their chief item of food. At times their crops were often destroyed by wild animals and sometimes seized by robbers. At other times they suffered from drought, which usually led to famine and pestilence.

Kings partly helped the people to overcome these difficulties. With the troops they employed to keep themselves in power, they checked invasions and suppressed rebellions. With the assistance of grades of officials whom they appointed over the various districts, they maintained peace and order. Utilizing rivers and large streams, they constructed huge tanks and extensive channels to provide the people with water for irrigating their fields. As Reginald Farrer points out in *In Old Ceylon*, the tanks were the pulsing hearts and the irrigation channels the arteries which carried life and nourishment to the wide cultivated fields which at that time covered the plains of the Dry Zone. Kings also assisted the religious bodies which helped people to lead good lives and prepare themselves for the attainment of happiness in the next life. The Buddhist *bhikshus* (monks) were believed to possess, like the Brahmin priest, the power to influence the elements and to prevent disasters over which ordinary human beings had no control.

Buddhism, which was introduced into Ceylon in the time of the great Emperor Asoka (c. 274-237 B.C.), supplied the spiritual and the cultural needs of the Sinhalese. Buddhist *vihārēs* (monasteries) came into existence in every important village, and served as centres of spiritual life, education and culture. The ruins of these in various parts of the island, many of them embellished by sculpture and painting, reveal the height to which Buddhism attained in this country and the extent of its influence over the people. Buddhism at first was mainly an other-worldly religion of the bhikshus. With the coming of Mahāyānism it became more popular and satisfied the needs of the laity better. Being monastic in form, it did not prevent the spread of the worship of Hindu gods, who replaced local deities and Mahāyānist *bōdhisattvas*. Thus while in India it was almost absorbed by Hinduism, in Ceylon it survived by expanding its own activities and allowing a lay Hinduism to supply the elements of popular religion it lacked. This religion and culture Ceylon derived from India. Hīnayāna or Thēravāda Buddhism came from the Empire of the Mauryas, Mahāyāna Buddhism from that of the Sātavāhanas, while Hindu influences reached Ceylon from the empires of the Guptas, the Pallavas and the Cōlas.

The caste system came to be gradually adopted during this period. Buddhism provided no organization for the laity as Christianity did. Society in Ceylon was at first mainly tribal. With the spread of Hindu ideas, tribe gave way to caste. Like tribe caste is based on kinship, and has the family and not the individual as its unit, but it has greater stability as it is supported by religious ideas and practices. Caste rests on the Hindu doctrines of *sva karma*, and the religious unity of the family. According to the doctrine of *sva karma*, the state of life into which a man is born is due to his actions in his previous births, and it is his duty to perform the obligations due from those of his status. The Brahmin priests performed rites not for congregations but for families, and thus strengthened the family system which saw that caste rules were observed and that individuals placed the interests of the family and of the caste before their own. The caste system specially suited agrarian and feudal conditions of life. In such a society a man's occupation normally depended on his birth and he had little chance of changing it. Hence the emphasis on birth seemed natural, and the hierarchy of castes according to occupations, like the hierarchies of gods and chiefs, was accepted.

The political history of this period was not uneventful. Ceylon was ruled at first by Devānampiya Tissa and his descendants and then by the Lambakarna and Mōriya dynasties. During the rule of the Mōriyas there was constant warfare, and finally there was a civil war between the descendants and followers of Sangha Tissa and those of Silāmeghavarna. The party of the latter finally triumphed, and after that there was on the whole internal peace up to the end of the Anurādhapura Period. The peace of the country was also disturbed by South Indian invasions, and for short periods South Indian adventurers ruled over this island. With the rise of the Cōlas, a great South Indian Empire came into existence, and Ceylon formed a part of it for over fifty years. Thereafter Polonnaruva, which the Cōlas made their seat of government, took the place of Anurādhapura as the capital of Ceylon. During this time there were wars among the rulers of Rajarata, Māyārata and Ruhuna, the three ancient provinces of Ceylon, but on the whole the factors that worked for unity prevailed, and except for short periods the Sinhalese continued to be united under a single sovereign.

Thus many features of our present civilization had their beginnings in the ancient period. The Sinhalese and the Tamils, the chief races of today, settled in the island during this time. Buddhism and Hinduism, which still have the largest number of adherents, became firmly established. The caste-system, which has persisted in a modified form up to the present day, took root during the Polonnaruva era. And the irrigation works, in which we are once more interested, were almost entirely a product of the ancient period.

2. THE MEDIEVAL PERIOD

The medieval period extended from the beginning of the thirteenth century to the end of the eighteenth. Politically Ceylon came to be divided during this time into three independent kingdoms. The invasion of Māgha, the final event of the civil war that followed the death of Parākramabāhu the Great, led to the establishment in the north of a Tamil Kingdom, which normally covered the present Northern Province. It survived the conquests of the Pāndya Empire, which took the place of the Cōla Empire in the thirteenth century, the Vijayanagara Empire, which came into existence in the fourteenth century, and the Kōttē Kingdom under Parākramabāhu VI, and came to an end only in 1621 when it was conquered by the Portuguese. Māgha's invasion forced the Sinhalese rulers to abandon the ancient centres of civilization like Anurādhapura and Polonnaruva as no man's land and gradually establish themselves in the south-west.

Parākramabāhu VI was the only Sinhalese king of this period who asserted his supremacy over the whole island. Most of the others were weak rulers and exercised little control over the semi-independent chiefs of the districts under them. This led to claims of political supremacy by powerful chiefs, civil wars, constant changes of capitals, and the rise at the end of the fifteenth century of an independent Kandyan Kingdom, which divided the Sinhalese politically into low-country and up-country. The Kandyan Kingdom covered the highlands, the present North-Central and Eastern Provinces and the Hambantota District. It survived the invasions of the kings of Sītāvaka, the Portuguese and the Dutch, and lost its independence only in 1815, with the occupation of Kandy by the British. The Sinhalese lowlands, covering the present North-Western, Western and Sabaragamuva Provinces and the Galle and Mātara Districts, formed the Kingdom of Kōttē in the fifteenth century. In the sixteenth century the government of this territory was shared by the kings of Kōttē and Sītāvaka until it fell into the hands of the Portuguese in 1597. The Dutch seized the Portuguese possessions in the middle of the seventeenth century, but for the greater part of the time they were in this island they had direct control mainly over the Jaffna Peninsula, the Western Province and the Galle and Mātara Districts.

The differences in these three kingdoms were not merely political. Distinctions arose in the economic sphere too. The Tamil Kingdom retained the ancient Dry Zone allodial system with its grain-tax, and the Portuguese and the Dutch when they occupied this area did not make any significant change in its economy. The Sinhalese kings, on the other hand, as they drifted to the Wet Zone allowed the irrigation works of the Dry Zone to go into decay. In the Wet Zone, where land suitable for the cultivation of paddy was limited, the freeholdings were gradually converted by kings into service lands, and thus the relations of the rulers with their subjects became feudal. The kings of this period obtained far less revenue than their predecessors who reigned in Anurādhapura and Polonnaruva, and they began to develop the foreign trade, especially in cinnamon. This trade brought Muslims in large numbers into the island. Later it led to the occupation of the Maritime Provinces by European powers. The Portuguese and the Dutch gradually modified the Sinhalese system of *rājakāriya*, or services due to the king, to suit the needs of their trade and government, but made no radical alterations in this Sinhalese form of feudalism. The Dutch improved the economic conditions especially in the Sinhalese areas. They repaired some of the tanks to help the cultivation of paddy. They developed communications by constructing canals. They established minor industries like carpentry and brick and tile-making. They encouraged the cultivation of commercial crops like coffee, and began the establishment of plantations which were to make great strides during the nineteenth century.

Socially too the differences in the three areas became more marked. In the Tamil area the South Indian forms of Hinduism and caste entrenched themselves strongly. In the Sinhalese districts too Hindu practices and caste ideas grew, but Buddhism, which suffered at first owing to constant wars, revived in the Kandyan Kingdom under the peaceful conditions that prevailed in the eighteenth century. Portuguese and Dutch rule increased further the differences between the low-country and the up-country peoples. The Portuguese introduced the Roman Catholic form of Christianity and the Dutch the Protestant, and a large section of the people of the lowlands became Christians. The Dutch went further in changing the ways of the people. They established a widespread system of elementary education which made a large section of the Sinhalese and the Tamils literate. They set up law courts, codified Tamil customs and applied Roman-Dutch Law where Sinhalese and Tamil customs failed to satisfy changing conditions. Thus they established the beginnings of the rule of law in this island. Above all they kept up Ceylon's contact with the West, established by the Portuguese, which today influences life in Ceylon at all points.

Thus the Dutch left the people of the coastal districts of the south-west and of the Jaffna Peninsula better prepared than the people of the rest of the island to take advantage of the developments that were to take place under the British.

3. THE MODERN PERIOD

The modern period may be said to begin with the British conquest of the Maritime Provinces in 1796. The British occupied the Kandyan Kingdom in 1815, and gained full control over it in 1818 by suppressing the rebellion which aimed at overthrowing their power. At the same time they began to establish in Ceylon a centralized form of government to which they were accustomed in their own country. They established, on the recommendation of the Colebrooke Commission, a common form of administration for the whole island, uniting the three separate administrative units of the Tamil, the Kandyan and the Low-country Sinhalese areas. The provinces were rearranged, uniting the Kandyan lowlands with the Low-country Sinhalese and Tamil districts. At the same time a common system of law courts was established for the whole island, bringing all persons under the rule of law and making them all equal in its sight.

Government after the Colebrooke reforms concerned itself, as it did in England at that time, with the maintenance of peace and order and justice and other elementary functions, and aimed at giving an impetus to change mainly by a reform of the laws. But in the absence of a powerful middle class as in England to undertake social and industrial activities, it had to perform certain other functions. To provide itself with men for the government services it established English schools. To help the development of the resources of the country and increase its revenue, it constructed roads and railways and restored irrigation works. From about 1870 it began, as it did in England at the time, to abandon its avowed *laisser-faire* policy, and to take more positive action to develop the resources of the country and improve the people and their condition. It began to provide elementary education for children and health and other services for the people, and from the beginning of this century it extended these services and made them much more effective.

When the British occupied Ceylon the economy of the people was on the whole agrarian. But the grain-tax and other sources of income such as the cinnamon monopoly did not produce a revenue sufficient to run a modern form of government with highly-paid European officials at the top. Therefore the British encouraged the opening of plantations in every possible manner. They abolished *rājakāriya*, which hindered the mobility of labour, and the government monopolies, which left little room for private enterprise and trade. From about 1837, owing to the increased demand for coffee in Europe, the number of coffee plantations quickly grew till they covered a great part of the hill country. But the cultivation of coffee was abandoned gradually in the seventies as the plants were attacked by a pest which could not be exterminated. The planters then took to the cultivation of tea. Later rubber and coconut plantations too were opened, and tea, rubber and coconut became the three major industries of the island.

The establishment of the plantations was accompanied by other developments. In the absence of Ceylonese capital and labour, it led to the introduction of European capital and Indian labour into this country. It led to the construction of roads and railways and of the Colombo harbour to facilitate the transport of their produce. It led to the growth of trade within the island and with foreign countries, and the village economy expanded into an international economy.

The administrative and economic developments brought about social changes. They led to the rise of government servants, lawyers, doctors, teachers, planters, traders, contractors, transport agents and businessmen. These came, especially in the Low-country Sinhalese areas, from all races and castes and formed the new middle class. The rise of this class led in turn to a weakening of caste ideas, the revival of Buddhism and Hinduism which suffered in the early part of British rule in their competition with Christianity, and a demand for constitutional reform.

Ceylon was at first given the form of Crown Colony government in which the Governor exercised supreme power subject only to the control of a distant Secretary of State and Parliament. In 1833 as a result of the recommendations of the Colebrooke Commission Ceylon was granted the form of Crown Colony government where the Governor, subject to the control of the Secretary of State and Parliament, ruled with the assistance of an Executive Council which he was bound to consult, and passed laws with the advice of a Legislative Council which included a minority of unofficial members.

In the nineteenth century there was a demand for the reform of the Legislative Council and it was asked for mainly by the unofficial European members. They asked not only for greater powers for the Council but also that the executive should be made responsible to the legislature. They failed to get a reformed Council but succeeded in getting some control of the budget. In the present century the demand for reform of the Council was by the new Ceylonese middle class whose leaders were influenced by British Liberal ideas, and they gradually gained complete control of the government by the changes made in 1912, 1921, 1924, 1931, 1947 and 1948. In 1912 the elective principle was conceded. In 1921 an unofficial majority was granted, and in 1924 full representative government. In 1931 the executive was made partly responsible to a legislature elected on an adult franchise. In 1947 full responsible government under the Crown in all matters of internal civil administration as well as some control over defence and external affairs was granted and in 1948 complete self-government within the British Commonwealth.

The British Period is undoubtedly the most important and the most interesting period of Ceylon History. It is certainly not colourful, and it has no history in the old sense of the term. But during it Ceylon has gone through greater changes than in all its previous history. The system of administration which was personal and feudal has given way to one highly centralized and modern. The agrarian economy has changed into a commercial. And the Crown Colony system has been transformed into a democratic and responsible form of government. But British rule has modernized only a small section of society, and one of the chief problems today is to bring the people as a whole into line with the administrative, economic and constitutional developments. British policy and methods of government have helped mainly the advancement of the people living in the south-western coastal districts and in the Jaffna Peninsula, and the rest of the island needs to be given more attention in the future if the country is to have a more uniform development. These and other problems created by British rule need to be solved, and to do this satisfactorily we have first to study the history of the British Period and understand the developments that produced them.

PART 1

FROM A MEDIEVAL TO A MODERN FORM OF GOVERNMENT

CHAPTER II

THE BRITISH OCCUPATION OF CEYLON

1. THE CONQUEST OF THE MARITIME PROVINCES

The British Period, may be said to have begun on the 15th February, 1796, when the Dutch Governor, Gerard van Angelbeek, surrendered Colombo, with the remaining Dutch territory in Ceylon and the dependencies in South India, to the superior British forces. The British had attacked Trincomalee on the 18th August, 1795, and conquered it eight days later. By the 6th October they had reduced all the fortresses along the coast northwards from Batticaloa to Mannār. Soon after this, five of the companies of the de Meuron regiment had left the service of the Dutch in Ceylon and joined the British in India. Van Angelbeek then withdrew his forces in Galle to strengthen the defence of Colombo. Finding it impossible to retain it, he accepted the terms offered by the British.

When the British East India Company came to trade in the East at the beginning of the seventeenth century, it was fully aware of the importance of the cinnamon of Ceylon. But it made no attempt to conquer the island because the Portuguese were well entrenched behind their fortresses. The Dutch, after they conquered the Maritime Provinces from the Portuguese, jealously guarded this source of wealth from the second half of this century. But before the middle of the eighteenth century their power had definitely declined. In Europe they had been reduced to a second-rate nation owing to their wars with the French; in the East their navy hardly counted when compared with those of the British and the French. But at this time the French were trying to oust the British from their trading posts in South-East India, and the British were kept too busy to think of the cinnamon trade in Ceylon which was monopolized by the Dutch. However in 1759 they became alive once more to the importance of Ceylon, but it was not for economic reasons.

At this time the British and the French were concerned mainly with the control of the eastern parts of India, and their sea fights took place in the Bay of Bengal. The east coast of India did not possess a single harbour which could be used as a naval base, and ships damaged in these battles had to be taken to Bombay for repairs. Moreover during the north-east monsoon, owing to the violent and dangerous hurricanes which blew at this time, ships had to be kept on the western side, leaving the eastern coast exposed to enemy attacks. In 1758 during the Seven Years' War, after a naval action with the French the British fleet retired to Bombay for repairs. During the north-east monsoon that followed, a French squadron appeared in the Bay of Bengal and assisted the land forces of the French in their siege of Madras. The British fleet could not return to the help of their countrymen till the monsoon changed in April.

These events made it clear to the British that a harbour had to be obtained in the Bay of Bengal. The best harbour was Trincomalee, which was not only spacious but also safe during both monsoons ; but this was in the possession of the Dutch. Therefore a harbour had to be sought on that part of the sea-coast which belonged to the King of Kandy. Fortunately for the British the King of Kandy, Kīrti Srī Rājasingha (1747-1782), appealed at this time for the aid of the Madras Government of the East India Company against the Dutch, and the Madras Government sent John Pybus in 1762 for the preliminary negotiations. Kīrti Srī offered a harbour and a share of the cinnamon trade, but nothing happened as the Madras Government refused to help him in return to expel the Dutch from Ceylon.

The Seven Years' War came to an end in 1763, and the British were engrossed in their own problems in India till the outbreak of the War of American Independence (1775-1783). When at the end of 1780 the Imperial Government declared war against the Dutch Republic, the East India Company found it a good opportunity to occupy Trincomalee. The Madras Government sent an embassy to Rājādhirājasingha (1782-1798) proposing an alliance with him to expel the Dutch from Ceylon, but he refused to treat with a government that did not help his brother in time of need. Nevertheless the East India Company occupied Trincomalee in 1782 ; but the French, who were also at war with the British and realized equally the value of this harbour, seized it from the British and restored it to the Dutch at the end of the war.

For another twelve years the British paid no attention to Ceylon till after the Revolution the French declared war against Britain on the 1st February, 1793. The French declared war against the Dutch Republic on the same day, entered its territories in October, 1794, and, after they had overrun the country in March, 1795, set up the Batavian Republic with the support of the pro-French party there. The Stadtholder William, who was also the commander-in-chief of the army of the Dutch Republic, fled to England, and sent a letter through the British to the Dutch Governor in Ceylon asking him in case of a French invasion to admit British troops to help the colonists who were loyal to him. The Madras Government did not want Trincomalee to fall into the hands of the French. Urged by the Imperial Government, it immediately sent an embassy to Rājādhirājasingha to seek his co-operation, and a fleet to conquer Ceylon if the Dutch refused to accept British protection.

What was the Dutch Governor to do? Dutch rivalry with the British in the past had been too acute for him to believe that the British, once they occupied Ceylon, would hand it back to the Dutch. Further the Stadtholder had not made it clear that he was to accept British protection. He therefore refused to place Ceylon under the British. Later when he learnt that the Batavian Republic had been established with the support of the majority of his countrymen, he decided to uphold its authority. This appears now to have been a short-sighted policy. Van Angelbeek no doubt knew the superiority of the British forces, but he probably expected that the French would come to his aid as they did before. He could also not have foreseen that the British would be finally victorious and that the only course of safety was to ally himself with them.

The British, for the safety of their possessions in India, had to occupy Ceylon. But for some time after the conquest the Imperial Government entertained the idea of returning Ceylon to the Dutch at the conclusion of the war. At the Peace of Amiens it changed its mind and decided to retain it as a British possession.

Thus came to an end the power of th Dutch whose rule was already decadent, and Ceylon fell into the hands of the British, the most progressive commercial and maritime power in Europe at the time.

2. THE FIRST WAR AGAINST KANDY

'Wherever a strong regularly governed state arises amidst a number of smaller powers, the latter are always likely to be absorbed by their great neighbour. Even when the great state harbours no designs of expansion, irritating events will from time to time lead it to intervene in the interests of its trade or in the general interests of good government'. So accounts Dodwell for British expansion in India.[1]

The British occupation of the Kandyan Kingdom was only a matter of time. A powerful, organized, modern power like the British, which had already occupied the Maritime Provinces by force, was bound to conquer the loosely-knit Sinhalese kingdom which was 'medieval' in every feature of its life. Besides the Kandyans too were bound to give cause for such action. The Portuguese had to invade Kandy as the Kandyan King allied himself with the Dutch to expel them from the low-country. The Dutch had attempted the conquest of the Kandyan Kingdom as the King sought the aid of the British against them. There was nothing to prevent the Kandyan King now from allying himself with the French to deprive the British of their recent conquests. In the rebellion[2] that took place against the Madras Government in 1797, the King definitely put his weight on the side of the rebels, and the British had to incur considerable expense in maintaining troops at strategic points along the frontier to prevent invasions from Kandy. Moreover the Kandyans were not likely to agree to terms satisfactory to the British. Although it was hoped that Trincomalee would be the chief naval base in the East, its hinterland did not provide the necessary supplies, and communications had to be established with Colombo. But the proposal to build a road from Colombo to Trincomalee through the Kandyan Kingdom was not only rejected but was looked upon with suspicion by the King, whose policy was to keep all Europeans out of his kingdom. One of the chief objects of the British was the expansion of their trade. But the import and export duties levied at the Kandyan frontier made trade with the highlands difficult. Therefore the British had either to gain control of the Kandyan Kingdom or conquer it to make their position in the lowlands secure and expand their trade.

1 *India*, Part I, by H. H. Dodwell, p. 83.
2 See page 31.

But the first step towards a treaty came from the Kandyans themselves. The Kandyan kingdom since 1739 had been ruled by South Indians. They were called Nāyakkars as they were the descendants of the Nāyakas or chiefs who ruled the districts of the Vijayanagara Empire. They were not popular with the semi-independent Sinhalese chiefs as their South Indian kinsmen dominated the court. But the rivalry of the Sinhalese chiefs, who were jealous of one another, maintained them in power. On the accession of Kīrti Srī there was a conspiracy to oust the Nāyakkars from the throne. Though it failed, the faction that aimed at placing a Sinhalese on the throne did not lose their power. At this time Pilimatalavvē, the chief Adigar, was the leader of the Sinhalese party, and he aimed at becoming king himself. At the death of Rājādhirājasingha he was not powerful enough to attain his object, and he placed on the throne Srī Vikrama Rājasingha, who, he expected, would be a tool in his hands. At the same time he exiled, imprisoned, or put to death all those who opposed his plans. After this he tried to obtain the support of the British to make himself king.

Frederick North (1798-1805), the British Governor at the time, had already recognised Srī Vikrama Rājasingha as king, and could not possibly entertain Pilimatalavvē's proposal. Nevertheless he was anxious to gain control of Kandy. At this time Wellesley, the Governor-General of India, found that many Indian states were in danger of being attacked by their more powerful neighbours. He offered to place within their territories British regiments for their protection, and formed treaties with them by which these states became subordinate to the British power in India. After his conversations with Pilimatalavvē, North believed that the King was in danger of his life, and he urged the Adigar to get the King to agree to a similar treaty by which a British regiment would be placed in Kandy. But the King was in no such plight. He had even ceased to be dependent on Pilimatalavvē and he was in no mood to become dependent on the British. There was no state from which he was in danger except the British themselves, and he refused to have anything to do with North's proposals in which he saw no advantage to himself.

But Pilimatalavvē did not give up hopes of becoming king. When he discovered that North would not help him, he tried to achieve his object by bringing about a war between the King and the British. He arranged for some Moors who were British subjects to be robbed of their arecanuts while trading in Kandyan territory. As he expected, North protested against the maltreatment of his subjects, and insisted that their losses should be made good. But the wheels of the Kandyan administrative system moved slow. The King had no control over all the actions of his chiefs. When he made no amends North rashly declared war against him, hoping by this means to force him to agree to the treaty that was rejected earlier.

North was not a practical man. He did not pause to think why the Portuguese and the Dutch failed to conquer the Kingdom of Kandy or bring the King under their control. It was true that the Kandyan army consisted of peasants who were ill-equipped and poorly trained. It could not resist well-armed, disciplined British troops. But the King of Kandy did not rely very much on his soldiers. He depended far more on the nature of the country and on a mode of warfare which suited the peculiar conditions of his territory.

According to Sinhalese conceptions the central part of the Kandyan Kingdom was a natural fortress in three ways. It was a *vana durga* and was difficult of access owing to the forests that surrounded it. It was a *giri durga*, and to enter it one had to ascend high mountains, rocks and sharp cliffs. During the rainy season it was a *jala durga*. Then the rivers rose, the forest tracks became almost impassable, and communication between the low-country and the highlands became very difficult.

The method of warfare among the Kandyans was not to give battle to the enemy in the open country. They knew they were powerless against well-equipped and well-trained European soldiers. They preferred to make surprise attacks in the jungle, where they were at an advantage owing to their knowledge of the country. The paths that led to the Kandyan Kingdom were so narrow that an invading army could proceed only in single file and found it difficult to overcome such opposition. If the enemy succeeded in reaching Kandy, they destroyed all supplies and retreated further inland. If they were followed, they tried to destroy the invaders by adopting the same tactics. In any case they allowed them to remain in Kandy till the rainy season in May, when the paths became impassable and supplies ceased to come. And then, taking advantage of the difficulties of the enemy, they forced them to surrender, or return and be attacked in the same way.

The British Army approached Kandy from two directions. It did not take the difficult route *via* Balanē by which the Portuguese attacked Kandy. One section, following the route taken by the Dutch Governor Van Eck, made its way through the Galagedara Pass, while the other marched from Trincomalee by way of Mātalē and the Ätgalla Pass. They met at Katugastota and occupied Kandy, but found that the King had retreated to Hanguranketa. Before long the British soldiers at Kandy suffered severely from malaria which they had contracted while marching through the jungle, and there were many casualties daily. The south-west monsoon then set in and communications with Colombo were interrupted. Suffering from sickness and scarcity of food, the British were soon in a helpless state and were compelled to surrender. In the end with a few exceptions they were massacred by the Kandyans.

Encouraged by this victory the King, according to the usual custom, attacked British territory in all directions. The British repelled these invasions; and, as the Portuguese and the Dutch did on similar occasions, sent expeditions into the Kandyan Kingdom destroying houses and crops. Sir Thomas Maitland (1805-1812), who succeeded North, put an end to these incursions, but he failed to come to any satisfactory arrangement with the King. Thus ended the war brought about by Pilimatalavvē's cunning and North's folly.

3. THE FALL OF KANDY

The War of 1803 was disastrous to the British and left the King in a stronger position. But on the other hand the British invasion of Kandy in 1815 received no serious opposition. The British Army, as the Portuguese did before, marched through Mattamagoda, Iddamalpāna, Hettimulla, Attāpitiya and Ganētänna, and reached Kandy by way of Balanē. The King fled on the approach of the British, and was captured at Bōmurē near Ūrugala and deported to South India.

Srī Vikrama Rājasingha realized that he had enemies not only without his kingdom but also within. He found that the main obstacle to the increase of his power as king lay near at home.

The Kandyan chiefs, who had continued to strengthen their position since the days of Rājasingha II, exerted considerable power over their districts. They possessed extensive *nindagam* over which they exercised almost sovereign power. They had ruled for generations, the son usually succeeding the father, though not necessarily over the same districts. Influenced by ideas of caste, the peasants believed that they were entitled to their posts by birth and looked upon them as their natural rulers. Most of the chiefs were allied by ties of kinship, and though they had their own differences could unite against a foreigner.

Srī Vikrama could not take any action against the chiefs as long as he had an enemy who was out to gain control over him. Now that British hostilities had ceased, he made it his policy to undermine their power. He began to entrust various duties hitherto performed by the chiefs to his Nāyakkar relatives. He rearranged and divided the districts over which the chiefs exercised a special influence. He appointed to vacant posts men who belonged to the junior branches of the great families, thus creating rivalry between the 'new men' and the other chiefs. He revived the *marāla*, a tax by which on the death of a chief a good portion of his property went to the state, and increased the fees which the chiefs had to pay whenever they received an appointment. He punished chiefs who oppressed their subjects and tried to win over the people to his side.

All these measures increased the hostility of the chiefs. Pilimatalavvē, who had so far failed to achieve his object, now planned assassination. But the conspiracy came to light, and the King put him to death in 1812. Ähälēpola succeeded him as the First Adigar and became the leader of the discontented chiefs. Whatever his own ambitions were, Pilimatalavvē had never been prepared to hand over the control of Kandy to the British. Had North realized this, he might not have declared war against the King. Ähälēpola on the other hand was vain and far less shrewd than his predecessor. In his desire to get rid of the King he soon began to fish in waters already abandoned by Pilimatalavvē.

Sir Robert Brownrigg (1812-1820), who succeeded Maitland, was sent with instructions to maintain friendly relations with the King of Kandy. The British policy in India at this time was to avoid extension of territory by conquest. Besides there was no longer any fear of an invasion of India by the French, and the

King had ceased at least for the time being to be a menace to the British occupation of the Maritime Provinces. But the British wanted to expand their trade. They wanted to strengthen their hold on Ceylon and improve the means of internal communication. Brownrigg too tried to make the King agree to a commercial treaty and failed. He began then to consider the conquest of the Kandyan Kingdom, and, like North, got into touch with the disaffected chiefs regardless of the propriety of his action.

When the King learnt of these intrigues between his chiefs and the British, he took steps against Ähälēpola and his supporters, and oppressed the people of the provinces which supported them. This drove Ähälēpola to seek direct aid against the King, but he found the British cautious after their disastrous Kandyan campaign of 1803. He realized that the only way he could get their support was by proving that there was sufficient opposition to the King. To demonstrate this he rose in rebellion, but as he received no help from the British he failed, and had to take refuge with his supporters in British territory.

The King was furious with his disloyal chiefs. In his eagerness for revenge he exceeded all bounds of humanity. He punished in most cruel ways the relatives of the chiefs who were kept as hostages at Kandy. He took steps even against bhikshus who were related to the disloyal chiefs, and in spite of the veneration in which they were held by the people, he executed one of them. These acts led to widespread discontent, and when the King tried to remove the families opposed to him from the Three and the Four Kōralēs, which lay between him and the British, there was open rebellion once more.

Brownrigg was now certain of conquering the King. He knew that he would succeed where others had failed. The King had antagonized the chiefs and he found that all of them welcomed British interference. Meanwhile some Sinhalese traders who were British subjects had been arrested as spies by the King's officers and sent back mutilated. The King's troops who defeated the rebels had pursued them into British territory and set fire to a village. Brownrigg considered these two acts sufficient provocation and declared war against the King.

Once Kandy was occupied, the British entered into a treaty with the Kandyan chiefs. The chiefs agreed to exclude the Nāyakkars from the throne and make the British king their sovereign. But the British were not able to get full control of the government. Since their victory was almost entirely due to the chiefs, they had to respect their rights, privileges and powers and to leave in their hands the criminal and civil jurisdiction over the districts they ruled. They also agreed to protect and maintain Buddhism, as they did not wish to rouse the opposition of the people by disturbing their religious susceptibilities. But the gains were not one-sided. The chiefs consented to the abolition of the customs duties levied at the frontier, thus helping the expansion of British trade. And the British by gaining control of Kandy made secure their hold over the island.

There are many interesting episodes connected with the Kandyan wars, some of which have led to much controversy. These have been omitted as they are not essential to the main story. Many mourn the loss of Kandy as it meant the extinction of Sinhalese rule which had lasted over two thousand years. But a medieval state, parochial in outlook like the Kandyan Kingdom, could not resist for long the advance of a modern imperial power like Britain, and the loss of independence was not without its compensations. Ceylon, which had been divided into a number of independent units for over three centuries, became at least politically united, and was soon assured of a period of peace and progress, free from foreign invasions and internal wars.

4. THE KANDYAN REBELLION

It did not take long for the chiefs to repent of their action. However tyrannical the king was, the Sinhalese feudal form of government rested lightly on the chiefs. In their own districts the chiefs acted like petty kings and their status and authority were fully accepted by the people. An organized modern government like that of the British was bound to become burdensome, however much their rights were recognized. The chiefs who ruled over the districts bordering the lowlands soon began to regret the loss of their frontier dues. All of them began to dislike the way the British administered justice. According to ideas of caste, the punishment meted out to a person depended not only on the crime committed but also on the status of the persons who committed it. But the British ignored caste distinctions and administered justice impartially, thus undermining the very foundations of the mode of life which gave the chiefs power and influence. Previously the chiefs had only the king above them. Now they had to take orders from British officials, and they did not receive from British soldiers the respect which they were accustomed to receive from their own people.

The chiefs were not the only persons who became dissatisfied. Buddhism at the time had become part and parcel of the feudal form of government that prevailed, and the bhikshus could not appreciate changes which reduced their power and influence. The king had not only taken part in religious ceremonies but had worshipped at the vihārēs and treated the bhikshus with great respect. But they found that the British officials could not take the place of the king, and that the British were not prepared to give them the veneration they were accustomed to receive. The people too did not appreciate the change. They had been accustomed to the Sinhalese form of government for generations and were too attached to their customs to abandon them lightly.

The chiefs who disliked British rule most were those of Bintänna and Vellassa. Under the Sinhalese kings the further a district was from the capital, the less interference was there with its chief. And these chiefs jealously guarded their rights. The Moors of this area got the British to appoint a Muslim Muhandiram over them to escape the levies of the Disāva. The Disāva naturally objected to the reduction of his income as well as his power, and when a pretender to the throne called Vilbāvē appeared in October 1817, he and his people supported him. Though there was no pre-arranged plan, once the revolt began the other chiefs who were dissatisfied joined the rebels, and before long only a few chiefs remained loyal to the British.

The British found the rebellion a formidable one. At this time most of the Kandyan country was covered with forest, and the rebels resorted as usual to guerilla warfare. They did not come into the open, but attacked the British troops as they traversed the jungle paths. It was found very difficult to crush the rebels, and at one stage the situation became so serious that the British burnt houses, destroyed crops, and damaged irrigation works in order to force the people into submission.

In the end the British succeeded in quelling the rebellion. The leading chiefs were jealous of one another and did not unite even in such an emergency. Molligoda, the chief of the Four Kōralēs, remained loyal, and the British were able to maintain communications between Colombo and Kandy. In the later stages the differences between the rebel chiefs undermined their power of resistance. Moreover the British forces, at first insufficient to subdue rebels who carried on guerilla warfare, were reinforced from India with troops and coolies to carry their supplies and war materials. Finally the recovery by the British, in November, 1818, of the *daladā* stolen at the beginning of the rebellion, persuaded the superstitious that the British could not be defeated. The Sinhalese believed that the possession of this relic of the Buddha gave its possessor the right to rule over the country.

Once the rebellion was supressed, the power of the chiefs was reduced and the subjugation of the Kandyan Kingdom was completed. The government of the Kandyan Provinces was brought directly under the British officials. Though the separate system of administration was continued the whole of Ceylon, which had become a single political unit three years earlier, now came under a similar system of government.

5. FORTRESSES AND ROADS

The British acquired the Maritime Provinces by conquest and had to retain them by the power of the sword. There was no danger of the Dutch re-capturing them, but there was every chance of the French expelling them once more from the island. The decisive sea battle of Trafalgar had not yet been fought, and there was nothing to prevent a French fleet coming to the East for the invasion of India.

The British at first adopted no new methods to establish their hold over Ceylon. In order to secure the trade of Colombo, the Portuguese had built there in 1518 a fortress similar to a medieval castle, the type of fortress which existed in Europe at this time. In the seventeenth century they had built other fortresses of a more advanced type at strategic points on the coast to protect themselves against European rivals. The Dutch had improved these and built others in the style they were built in Europe in the seventeenth century. They had fortresses at Mullaitīvu, Trincomalee, Batticaloa and Pānama in the east, Jaffna in the north, Mannār, Kalpitiya, Puttalam, Negombo, Colombo and Kalutara in the west, and Galle, Mātara, Tangalla and Hambantota in the south. The British repaired and garrisoned these fortresses. They made Trincomalee their naval and military headquarters, and through it they hoped to control the Indian Ocean and to protect India against an attack from sea.

When the Kandyan Kingdom was occupied, the British followed the methods of defence used by the Portuguese and the Dutch. The Portuguese and the Dutch had established military posts at strategic points along the Kandyan frontier to resist invasion. The British now did the same at important points within the Kandyan provinces to maintain their conquest. They stationed troops on the old route from Colombo to Kandy, at Ruanvälla, Iddamalpāna, Hettimulla, Attāpitiya and Amunupura at the top of Balanē Pass, at Kurunāgala and Galagedara on the route from the north-west which the British took during their first war against Kandy ; at Nālanda and Ätgalla on the way from Trincomalee through Mātalē. In order to make themselves more secure they built fortresses at Amunupura, Galagedara and Atgalla, the chief passes, and established a depot for the supply of goods at Ruanvälla. They placed troops also at Kandy and Badulla, the chief towns and natural fortresses of the Kandyan Kingdom, and at Batugedara (near Ratnapura), the most important place from a strategic point of view between Colombo and Badulla. They also cleared the forest along the tracks between the low-country and the highlands to safeguard communications, and made a map of the interior to help the movement of troops.

After the Kandyan rebellion was stamped out and the British gained a firmer hold of the Kandyan provinces, they kep troops along the three main routes at Ruanvälla and Fort King (Attāpitiya), Kurunāgala and Galagedara, and at Fort Macdowall (Mātalē), as well as at strategic points like Kotmalē (between Nāvalapitiya and Talāvakällē), Maturata (south of Hanguranketa), and Nuvara Eliya ; Ratnapura, Badulla, Fort Macdonald (near Välimada) and Alupota (south-east of Passara).

Sir Edward Barnes (1820-1830), who succeeded Brownrigg, was the first to adopt new methods. He did not approve of the use of fortresses for maintaining the British hold on Ceylon. Most of the military posts were in malarial districts, and many soldiers suffered from fever and died. The British Government in England, after the Rebellion of 1745, had built military roads in the highlands of Scotland as a protection against further Jacobite risings. Besides in England at this time a large number of roads had been made, and the importance of the work of Metcalfe, Telford and Macadam

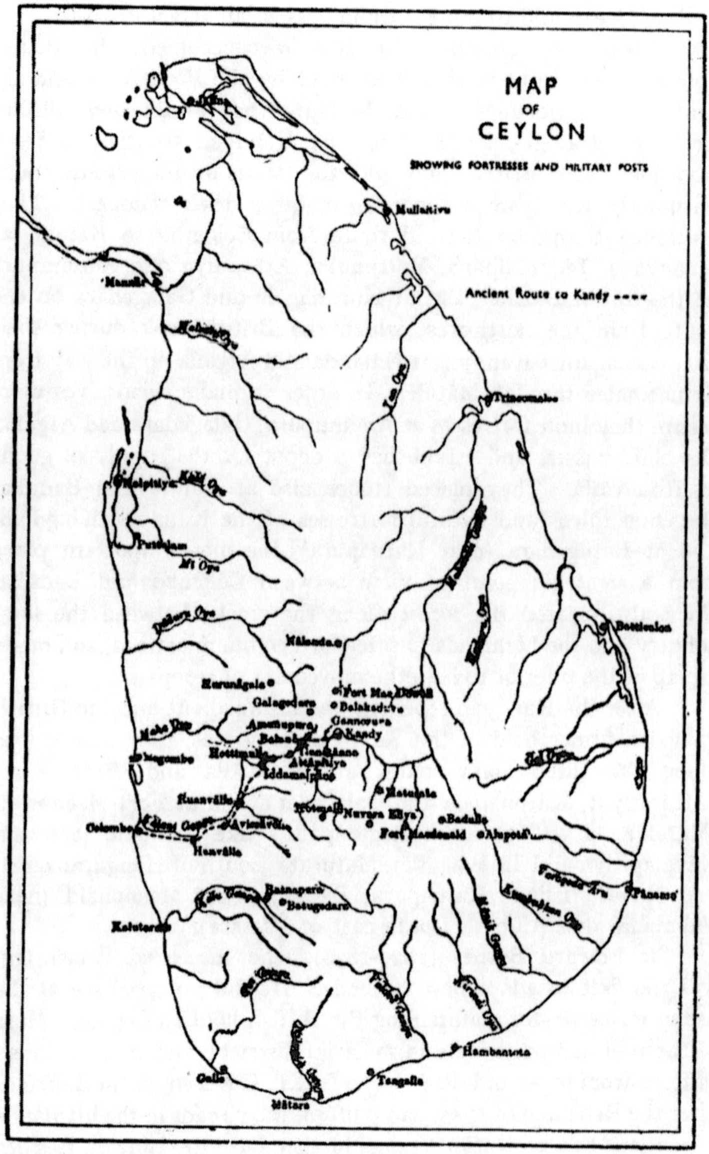
MAP
OF
CEYLON
SHOWING FORTRESSES AND MILITARY POSTS
Ancient Route to Kandy
Mullaitivu
Mannār
Trincomalee
Kalpitiya
Puttalam
Batticaloa
Nālanda
Kurunāgala
Fort MacDowall
Galagedara
Kandy
Negombo
Colombo
Badulla
Nuvara Eliya
Fort Macdonald
Ratnapura
Kalutara
Hambantota
Galle
Tangalla
Mātara

was being realized. Barnes decided to abandon the fortresses and link Kandy by roads, along which troops could move quickly with their cannon in case of revolts.[1]

In 1820 Barnes began to build a road from Colombo to Kandy. It was opened for traffic in 1821, the gravelling was finished in 1825, and it was completed in 1832. This road did not follow the ancient route which went along the Kälani Ganga via Hanvälla, Avissāvēlla and Ruanvälla and then through Iddamalpāna, Hettimulla, Attāpitiya, Balanē and Gannoruva. It took a more direct route through Kälaniya, Mahara, Heneratgoda, Vēyangoda, Pasyāla, Varakapola and crossed the old road near Ganētänna. After this in order to maintain a satisfactory gradient for vehicles, it zigzagged keeping to the side of the hill and reached the summit at Kadugannāva. This part of the road was constructed by Captain Dawson, and on his death the tower at Kadugannāva was built to commemorate his work. In 1821 Kurunägala was connected with Kandy via Galagedara Pass, and in 1825 it was further linked with Colombo by a road from Ambēpussa on the Colombo-Kandy Road. This road was extended to Dambulla in 1827. In 1831 a road was built from Kandy to Mātalē and extended to Dambulla in 1832, meeting the road from Colombo via Kurunägala. Thus roads traversed all the three passes to Kandy at Kadugannāva, Galagedara and Atgalla, and made it possible to reach the centre of the island quickly from three directions.

All these roads were not very different from the Dutch track along the coast. They were rough clearings through forests and had no permanent bridges or culverts. The approaches to rivers and streams were graded to enable carts to cross them in ferry boats. The only exceptions were the road from Colombo to Kandy and the one which branched off from Ambēpussa to Kurunägala where bridges were built. On the Kandy Road a bridge of boats was constructed in 1822 over the Kälani Ganga at Grand Pass.

1 Roads were not a new feature in Ceylon. They existed within the limits of the towns. The Dutch had made a wide track along the coast round the island, and by 1814 the British had improved the part between Colombo and Galle. Brownrigg had planned a road from Colombo to Trincomalee, and would have begun its construction but for the Kandyan rebellion. With the end of the wars in Europe in 1815 the importance of Trincomalee had waned, and there was not the same urgency to establish land communication between it and Colombo.

Three other bridges were built on the fifty-ninth mile, on the sixty-seventh mile over the Nānuoya, and at Māvanälla. Over the Mahaväli Ganga at Pērādeniya a bridge of satinwood was completed in 1832.

It was possible to build so many roads in such a short time as Government had not to incur much expenditure over them. Before the British occupation every male inhabitant of the island had to render free a fortnight's labour to Government for the repair of the paths and the bridges of his district. The British Government utilized this *rājakäriya*[1] for the opening of roads and employed military officers to trace them and supervise the work of the labourers.

It was not the military alone that found these roads of value. This was the age of stage-coaches in England. Carriages drawn by horses were already in use in Colombo.[2] In December 1831 the Governor and a number of government servants formed a company to run a mail coach between Colombo and Kandy, and thus the first mail coach in Asia was started in 1832. The fare was £2 10s *od*, or about Rs. 25, but the comfort and the speed of the new mode of travel more than made up for the high cost.

The roads contributed also to the development of the Postal Department. The British Government at the commencement of its rule established a postal system for the conveyance of official letters. It set up post offices at Colombo, Trincomalee, Jaffna, Mannār, Galle and Mātara, and the letters were carried daily from these stations by runners. The Postal Department now utilized mail coaches and other vehicles for the despatch of letters, and employed runners only in areas where there were no roads

It has been seen how Ceylon became a single political unit with the conquest of the Kandyan Kingdom and how an administrative system similar to that of the Maritime Provinces was adopted in Kandyan territory after the suppression of the Rebellion. Roads helped to further this unification. They broke down the isolation of a large number of villages and brought many districts into closer touch with Colombo, while the Postal Department utilized them to send out information from Colombo to various parts of the island.

1 See Ch. IV, Section 4.

2 Such carriages however were unknown in Kandy. The Kandyan ambassadors who visited North, when conveyed in one of these, insisted on the doors being kept open during the journey lest they be mistaken for prisoners!

CHAPTER III

ADMINISTRATIVE DEVELOPMENT (1796-1832)

1. THE GOVERNMENT OF THE EAST INDIA COMPANY AND DUAL CONTROL

The conquest of the Maritime Provinces of Ceylon by the Madras Government made it inevitable that the territory held by the Dutch should come under its control. Though all conquests of the East India Company were made in the name of the King of Great Britain, the Imperial Government could not take over the administration immediately. The East India Company had spent a considerable sum of money in the conquest and therefore had some claim to the revenue and trade of Ceylon.

But the change was most unfortunate. The Madras Government had not yet evolved a satisfactory form of government even for its own territory. South India had suffered from anarchy and strife, and it was still governed to some extent according to methods adopted by irresponsible adventurers. The methods of revenue-collection for instance were most oppressive. The taxes were farmed, and those who undertook the collection tried to squeeze as much as possible from the peasants. There was no question of ownership of land in those days, and lands were not sold for non-payment of taxes. What mattered was the crop, and the aim of the farmer of taxes was to get the maximum share for Government. If he failed to secure it by peaceful means, he resorted even to torture.

The Madras Government entrusted the administration in Ceylon at first to military officers, but soon made arrangements to collect taxes and control the trade of the island. It divided the Maritime Provinces into three and placed each part in charge of a British official. The Indian word *kachcheri* which we still use was the name they gave to their offices. But when it came to the collection of revenue the new Government found many obstacles. The system of land-tenure to which they were accustomed was very different from that of the Sinhalese. It was more akin to the system that prevailed among the Tamils in the north of Ceylon. The Tamils who held land rendered no services on that account. Instead they paid one tenth of the produce of their fields and gardens, and this the officers of Government collected at harvest time.

The Sinhalese system was quite different. There were certain villages which came directly under the Dutch Company. These were the *gabadāgam* of the Sinhalese kings which supplied the food of the King's household. Each of these contained a large field which belonged to the Company ; and the inhabitants of the place, instead of paying rent for the land they occupied, either cultivated it or performed other services for the Company. Some villages of this type were held by individuals, who had received them as gifts or as payment for services rendered to Government. They were called *nindagam* ; and the owner or lord not only received the services of the people but also acted as their ruler. He settled all disputes among his tenants and punished those who were guilty of minor offences or crimes.

Lands other than *nindagam* were also given for services. The Company had employed men to guard the coasts, frontiers and roads, to maintain peace and order, to defend the country in time of war, to carry provisions and stores, to clear jungles, to dig canals, to make roads, and to peel cinnamon. These men were not paid for such work but were given lands called *vädavasam*. One male of every family that enjoyed such a holding had to work for three months for Government. If he worked outside his district he was paid *batta* or a daily allowance.

The Madras Government, even if it tried, could not have worked through its officers this complicated system of services. It adopted a simpler method. It abolished the Sinhalese land-tenure system and asked the people to pay instead half the produce of their fields. It believed that when the people became the owners of their lands, they would take more interest in their development, and thereby it would receive a larger share of revenue. It imposed in addition a number of new taxes. For instance it ordered owners of coconut lands which contained fifty trees or more to pay a tax of two pence per tree.

The Madras Government went further. In the years preceding the British conquest, the Mudaliyārs were the chief military and civil officials of the districts. They collected taxes, exacted the services due to the Company, helped to ttle civil disputes and to punish criminals, carried out the orders of the Dutch officials, and kept them informed of what was going on in the country. In short they possessed great powers and formed an *imperium in imperio*. The Madras Government feared that they would be a serious obstacle to its rule. Therefore it relieved them of their duties, and took away from them the *nindagam* which had been granted to them for their services. It gave the posts rendered vacant to South Indian officers called Amildars, and the lower posts to other officers that came with them.

The Sinhalese people did not approve of the change. They had been accustomed to the system of services since the days Sinhalese rulers had moved from the Dry Zone to the Wet Zone in the south-west. The Portuguese and the Dutch had allowed them to continue this "feudal" form of land-holding, and they desired no change. They objected even more to the new taxes and the way the revenue was collected. The practice at this time was to farm or sell the collection of taxes by auction to the highest bidder. Under the Madras Government the right of collection was bought by these Indian officials and their followers, who were ignorant of the customs of the people and had no interest in their welfare. They harassed the people and took from them much more than they had a right to levy. The people were helpless against these exactions. The Amildars not only collected revenue but also acted as judges, and the people could not go before them to complain against their own actions and those of their subordinates.

The discontent and suffering that followed these sudden changes in the people's relations to Government and the acts of oppression of its officers led to a revolt in 1797. Ceylon at this time was a land of villages, and the villages were usually in places such as valleys where a supply of water could be obtained for the cultivation of rice. The rest of the country was generally covered with forest. The rebels kept to the jungle and attacked British forces from their hiding places, and the British could not subdue them till March 1798. The revolt was no doubt engineered by the Mudaliyārs, who not only lost their posts and the *nindagam* which gave them power and wealth, but also had to pay various new taxes such as that on coconut trees.

The revolt made the Madras Government realize the mistake of introducing suddenly changes in government to which the people were not accustomed. It abolished the coconut-tax to which there had been much objection, and charged instead an export duty on coconuts. It restored the right to retain lands for services, dismissed the Indian officials, and gave back to the Mudaliyārs the posts they held earlier. In short it went back more or less to the form of government that had prevailed in the days of the Dutch and to which the Sinhalese had been long accustomed.

It is not possible to say how the Imperial Government would have viewed the mistakes of the Madras Government. In November 1797, before news of the revolt reached London, it decided not to give Ceylon back to the Dutch in any case immediately, and thought of taking over the government of Ceylon from the Company. The Company expressed its unwillingness to give up Ceylon as Trincomalee harbour was necessary for the protection of India. So the Imperial Government placed Ceylon in the position of an Indian Presidency such as that of Bombay and shared its control with the East India Company. According to this arrangement the Governor was to be appointed by the Crown and was to be under the direction of the Governor-General of Bengal and the Board of Directors. He was to exercise all legislative, executive and military authority but without an advisory council of the type that existed in the Presidencies. The personnel of the Civil Service was to be under the Governor, but those employed for purposes of supervising the collection of revenue and the control of trade, including the cinnamon monopoly, which were to be the concern of the East India Company, were to be recruited from the Company's service in Madras. Apart from this the form of government underwent little change. The higher posts were held by the British and the Company's officials, while the administration of the kōralēs was left in the hands of the Mudaliyārs and their assistants. The British policy at this time was to leave unchanged the ancient institutions of the peoples of their colonies unless considerations of humanity demanded their alteration or abolition.

The new system of government satisfied the chiefs, but it proved a failure from an administrative point of view. The officials who came from Madras were neither honest nor efficient. Their training did not help them to govern Ceylon as the customs and the languages of the people of South India differed from those of the Sinhalese. The Madras officials also worked against North, who was sent from England in 1798. They did not favour his appointment as they believed that the post should be filled by one of themselves.

The arrangements made in 1796 were therefore discontinued, and the unfortunate connection of the East India Company with the British Government in Ceylon was brought to an end. On the 1st January, 1802 the British possessions in Ceylon were made a Crown Colony, and were brought directly under the control of the Imperial Government.

2. THE CHIEFS AND THE CIVIL SERVICE

When the connection of the British East India Company with the administration in Ceylon ceased, the Governor became the chief authority over the Maritime Provinces. He became the chief executive officer and legislative authority. He was given a council of officials to advise him on the more important matters, but he was not bound to consult it or follow its decisions. He had to answer for his actions only to the Secretary of State, and through him to the British Parliament; but at this time a communication to England took nearly six months to reach London, and the Governor was generally given a free hand except in formulating policy, which the Secretary of State dictated in all important affairs.

Under the new system of government the Maritime Provinces were divided into eight districts and each of them was placed under an Agent of Revenue. It was too expensive to get men from England to do the clerical work in offices, and the posts of clerks were given to the Burghers, who proved a valuable link between the British officials and the inhabitants of the towns.

The failure of the Madras officials and Government's own experience showed that it was necessary to have not only a more efficient but also a larger Civil Service. The Civil Servants in Ceylon, unlike those in England, had numerous duties to perform. They had, for instance, to see to the entire collection of revenue. They were the chief executive and judicial authorities in their districts, and had to act as if they were the rulers of their areas. So the efficiency of Government depended on the efficiency of the Civil Service. The British Government therefore increased the number of posts in the Civil Service to forty-five, and took steps to attract good men to fill them. If offered pensions to all who joined the Service and promised them regular promotions. By these methods it hoped to induce them to spend their whole career in Ceylon and acquire a good knowledge of local conditions.

The British Government realized from the outset that it could not get an adequate hold of the country by these steps alone The Sinhalese and the Tamils were not advanced enough for a bureaucratic form of government. The only form of government they appreciated was a paternal one in which the officials personally saw to their needs and redressed their grievances. Being foreigners the British officials could not get into personal touch with the peasants, and had to depend on the Mudaliyārs for all information regarding the country. The result was that the government of the country virtually remained in the hands of the Mudaliyārs.

In order to change this state of affairs and make British rule secure, British Governors began to devise methods to reduce the powers of the Mudaliyārs and to bring the Civil Servants into close touch with the people. North took back the *nindagam* given to the Mudaliyārs for their services and deprived them of the sovereign powers which they exercised in such villages. Instead he paid them salaries, and made them dependent on Government for their maintenance. Maitland, who established the British system of administration in Ceylon on a firm foundation, g ve up many of North's schemes of reform, but followed him with regard to Mudaliyārdom and the Civil Service. In order to curtail the powers of the Mudaliyārs further he relieved them of their judicial work, and entrusted it to Magistrates whose number he increased.[1] He appointed Vidānēs to do police duty in the villages, but placed them under the supervision of the Justices of the Peace[2] and not of the Mudaliyārs. He entrusted the keeping of *thombos*, the registers of land revenue, to schoolmasters so that the British officials might have another source from which they could obtain information about the country. He began to fill the posts of Mudaliyārs, which generally went from father to son, with members of other important families, and weakened the influence of the older ruling families. In the Civil Service he found that the private trade carried on by

1 For the development of a system of paid magistrates in Britain, see Keir: *The Constitutional History of Modern Britain*, p. 389.

2 The Justices of the Peace at this time were either magistrates, or officials who could exercise magisterial powers.

its servants, following the example of the officials of the East India Company, interfered with their official duties, and that some other activities in which they took part led to corruption. He forbade Civil Servants to engage in private trade and took steps to prevent corrupt practices. He offered rewards to Civil Servants who acquired a knowledge of Sinhalese as it enabled them to get into personal touch with the peasants. He realized that a government carried on from an office would not be successful, that the tent was mightier than the pen, and ordered officials in charge of districts to make frequent circuits in order that they might find out the needs of the people.

Brownrigg followed the same policy in the Kandyan Provinces. When they were occupied in 1815, he appointed a Resident and four officials to govern them. Though at first he was obliged to leave the districts in the hands of the chiefs, in 1818 after the suppression of the Rebellion he divided the Kandyan territory into eleven districts and placed each of them under a Government Agent. He increased the number of Civil Servants and took steps to bring them into closer touch with the people. He deprived the chiefs of their *nindagam* and paid them salaries. He reduced their judicial work and abolished the judicial fees they received from the people. Barnes and Sir Robert Wilmot Horton (1831-1837) took further steps to improve the efficiency of the Civil Service. Barnes refused to promote an assistant Civil Servant unless he possessed a good knowledge of Sinhalese or Tamil, while Horton in 1832 ordered Civil Servants to learn both Sinhalese and Tamil.

Thus the British succeeded where the King had failed. They had the necessary power to enforce their measures, and a new body of men to be entrusted with the powers they took away from the chiefs. The chiefs had no external power to appeal to for help, and had to reconcile themselves gradually to their lot.

3. THE JUDICIARY

We have seen the difficulties experienced by the British in ruling a people whose political ideas and economic conditions, as well as languages and social customs, were different. The establishment of a satisfactory judicial system proved even more complex. The Dutch had undoubtedly established a judicial system suited to the conditions of the people. They had set up three kinds of law courts. They had codified the civil laws of the Tamils, the *Tēsavalamai*. They had introduced Roman-Dutch Law to be applied in the case of the Burghers, and when local laws were not clear on any point they had extended its application to the people of the country.

The British found it difficult to take over the work of the law courts as they were ignorant of Roman-Dutch Law and of local customs. According to the terms of capitulation the Dutch judges dealt with the cases which were pending at the time of the British conquest. When they were asked to continue they refused, but when they realized that Ceylon would not be handed back to the Dutch they agreed to resume their work.

When North became Governor, he established a Supreme Court in place of the Dutch *Raad van Justitie* and himself acted as the chief judge. He set up civil courts in the chief towns and revived the Dutch *Landraads* to deal with civil cases in rural areas. He also established Civil Courts of Appeal so that those dissatisfied with the decisions of the civil courts might get their cases re-tried.

When Ceylon became a Crown Colony there were further changes. A Supreme Court of Judicature was established and British barristers were appointed as judges relieving North and his officials. It exercised criminal jurisdiction over the Maritime Provinces and civil jurisdiction over all persons within Colombo and over all Europeans within British territory. The minor criminal cases were dealt with by Magistrates and the Justices of the Peace. And provincial courts were established to exercise civil jurisdiction over the Ceylonese.

According to British practice at this time, there was a separation of judicial and executive authorities to safeguard the liberty of the subject. This practice was maintained in Ceylon as far as the Europeans were concerned. But as British lawyers were not acquainted with the conditions of the country or the institutions of the people, which at the time it was their policy to maintain, the provincial courts were presided over by the executive officials and their work was supervised by the Governor who acted also as the President of the High Court of Appeal. The ignorance of Sinhalese and Tamil on the part of lawyer-judges led to mistakes even in criminal cases. These were partly avoided by the introduction in 1811 of trial by jury. The jurors knew local conditions and could detect mistakes made in the process of translation.

The dual system of courts, one under the Supreme Court and the other under the Governor, did not work satisfactorily. Both the Governor and the judges were very jealous of their rights. Each objected to the interference of the other, and the absence of any division of their powers often led to clashes. One such case took place in the time of Barnes. The Collector of Jaffna ordered a slave who got himself carried in a palanquin to be flogged. The Supreme Court quashed the sentence as neither Dutch nor British law decreed flogging in such a case. Barnes disapproved of the interference of the Supreme Court, and to justify the action of his subordinate passed a regulation authorizing the flogging of a slave for any offence.

But there was no solution to these conflicts. As long as the Sinhalese feudal economy prevailed, it was not possible to bring the provincial courts under the Supreme Court. Even the meticulous Dutch had failed to codify the Sinhalese customs, and the British could not do it in a short time. Hence the settlement of disputes among the Sinhalese had to be left to the officials, who through their administrative work got into touch with the people and learnt their habits and customs.

CHAPTER IV

SOCIAL AND ECONOMIC CHANGES (1796-1832)

1. HUMANITARIAN ACTIVITIES AND THE GRANT OF RELIGIOUS TOLERATION

The British policy at this time was to foster the welfare of the people of their colonies. At the time the Dutch held the Maritime Provinces, rulers in Europe had greatly improved upon the manner in which they treated their subjects. They were giving up cruel and barbarous punishments and trying to improve the lot of their people. Sinhalese kings and chiefs, as we have seen already, often tortured people as medieval-European rulers did, and deprived them of their limbs for acts of sedition and other serious crimes. The Portuguese and the Dutch had not abstained from inflicting similar punishments. But during the eighteenth century the Dutch, influenced by the humanitarian movement in Europe, had punished two of their governors for inhuman acts and executed one of them. The British, who were deeply influenced by the same movement, abolished the practice of mutilation and torture soon after they conquered the Maritime Provinces. In 1815 they insisted on the abolition of these and other inhuman practices that prevailed within the Kandyan Kingdom.

The British Government went much further. At this time people of the upper classes in Europe were taking an interest in the well being of the poor, and of backward peoples in other parts of the world. They demanded the abolition of slavery and the improvement of the conditions of the poor in an outside Europe. The British were in the van of these movements and so took steps to end slavery in Ceylon. The Dutch had recognized slavery and had employed slaves as servants in their homes. Whenever their household furniture was auctioned, usually their slaves were also sold. In the Tamil districts there were three castes of people who were treated more or less as slaves. In the Kandyan Provinces too there were slaves, though they were treated as dependents and were entitled to certain privileges. The British at first tried to discourage slavery. North, out of sympathy, favoured slaves in their disputes with their masters. In response to British suggestion, in

1816 the Burghers offered to set free the children of their slaves. Brownrigg took advantage of the offer in 1818, and made it further possible for slaves who wanted to free themselves to purchase their freedom. In 1821 Barnes passed a regulation which gave the Government power to purchase from their masters all female slave children born after 24th April. But slavery in Ceylon was not abolished in 1833 as in most other parts of the British Empire. The British in India were reluctant to interfere with religious and social customs, and slavery in Ceylon was ended only when it was abolished in India in 1844.

The British showed their humanitarianism in other ways too. In 1800 there was an outbreak of smallpox. The usual practice in Ceylon at this time was to segregate the smallpox patients in a hut in the jungle adjoining the village: or, if the epidemic was serious, to abandon the village leaving the patients behind with those, if any, who were immune from the disease. According to Skinner[1] many of these patients were attacked by wild beasts and torn to pieces. North disapproved of the methods adopted by the Sinhalese. He ordered the establishment of hospitals at the four principal stations for the treatment of smallpox, and appointed overseers to deal with cases in the villages.

North did not stop with this. He made use of one of the discoveries made in Europe during the eighteenth century. Since early times, it was known that after recovery from a disease a patient often became immune from further attacks. In the East this had led to the inoculation of children with the virus from mild smallpox cases, and the slight attack which followed had conferred lasting protection against severe forms of the disease. In 1796 the Englishman, Jenner, discovered that an attack of cow-pox gave the same immunity. Two years later he recommended vaccination with the serum obtained from the diseased cow, and thus made precautionary measures against smallpox possible on a large scale. In 1802 North introduced this form of vaccination and reduced the mortality and frequency of smallpox in Ceylon.

Europe had progressed in other directions too. In the eighteenth century European rulers had begun to realize the futility of religous persecution and to allow their subjects freedom of

1 Thomas Skinner, the great road-maker of Ceylon. His *Fifty Years in Ceylon* is valuable for the study of the History of the British Period.

worship. In India and Ceylon it had not been the custom to punish people for following any faith they liked. No Indian religion was organized like the Christian churches on a national or even provincial basis, or offered any opposition to those in power ; and kings, instead of persecuting a particular faith, granted favours to all. In Europe on the other hand the Church was organized and at times kept even rulers in check ; and rulers generally tolerated only those who followed their faith.

The Portuguese did not persecute anyone in Ceylon, though they made every effort to convert rulers and people to Roman Catholicism even by offering worldly advantages. On the other hand the Dutch at first tried hard to prevent Buddhists, Hindus, Muslims and Roman Catholics from carrying on religious worship in public places and withheld from them the civil rights granted to the Protestants. But influenced by the change of view in Europe, they began to relax their regulations in the latter part of the eighteenth century. The British had granted religious toleration to Roman Catholics in Great Britain, and the early British rulers did not enforce the Dutch laws against them. Maitland not only repealed these laws in 1809 but also went further and granted the Roman Catholics the privileges enjoyed by the Protestants in order to win their support for British rule. Perhaps he was influenced by the fact that in India the Roman Catholics and the Protestants had enjoyed the same privileges from the time Bombay was given to Charles II as dowry by Portugal.

Thus though the people of Ceylon suffered certain disadvantages by the British occupation, they also benefited from the enlightened outlook of their new rulers.

2. EDUCATION

When the British established a more advanced and enlightened form of government in Ceylon, they should also have tried to raise the intellectual standard of the people to enable them to appreciate and benefit by the changes they made. But little was done in this direction, and this is not surprising. At the time it was not realized even in England that the education of the masses was a national responsibility. And they could not do more for the people of Ceylon than for their own people. Nor did they realize sufficiently that the peasants of Ceylon were not in a position to adjust themselves to the new political conditions.

The Dutch had been ahead of the British in matters of education. They were Presbyterians and their Reformed Churches, which cared little for religious ceremonial, stressed the responsibility of each man directly to God for his acts. They undertook the education of the people to enable them to read the Bible and other religious books. When the Dutch occupied Ceylon, the Reformed Church established schools throughout the Maritime Provinces. The children were taught reading, writing and the Christian religion. The Government of the Dutch East India Company maintained these schools for political reasons too. It believed that those whom the Church converted to Christianity would be more loyal to their rule.

The British East India Company did not consider it its duty to spread Christianity in Ceylon. In fact it feared that Christian propaganda would disturb its trade, and for two years it neglected the schools. North acted differently. He was influenced by high humanitarian motives and looked upon education at least as an instrument for the moral improvement of man. He was influenced by political motives too. He feared that if those who had become Christians under the Dutch went back to Buddhism and Hinduism, they would become hostile to the British. So he revived the schools. Like the Dutch, he employed European clergymen and Ceylonese catechists to supervise the work of the schools, for in England at this time education was carried out by the Church. The practical Dutch had maintained the teachers by giving them as their wages the fees of marriages performed in their schools. North did not approve of fees for solemnizing marriages. He abolished them and paid the teachers regular salaries. But it was soon discovered that Government had not the funds to pay these salaries, and from 1803 the schools fell into neglect once more.

The pressure for the revival of these schools came next from England. In the latter part of the eighteenth century there was a religious revival in England, and the Evangelical Movement which it produced influenced the middle classes of the Church of England. The leaders of this movement held views similar to those of the Dutch Presbyterians, and established Sunday schools and later day schools to spread elementary education. They also took an interest in human welfare. They led the movement for the abolition of the slave-trade, and worked for the spread of Christianity in non-Christian lands. When Wilberforce and other leaders of the movement learnt that Christians in Ceylon were relapsing into Buddhism and Hinduism owing to the neglect of the schools, they urged the Imperial Government to restore them. So in 1810 Maitland once more began to revive the schools. Brownrigg, who was interested in Christian educational work, opened a number of new schools. But Barnes did not approve of teaching Christianity to non-Christians. In 1820 he abolished the posts of catechists who supervised the work of the teachers, and the schools fell into neglect again.

In addition to the Sinhalese and the Tamil schools, North had established a seminary in Colombo. It consisted of an English school for European children, and a Sinhalese and a Tamil school for Sinhalese and Tamil children in which English was also taught. North also opened a few English schools in the towns to secure persons with a knowledge of English to man the government departments. These schools did not last long, but the demand for a knowledge of English remained as it was a qualification for employment under Government. Brownrigg opened about a dozen schools in various parts of the island, and entrusted them to Wesleyan missionaries, but Barnes stopped the allowances paid to the missionaries. The schools gradually disappeared after 1820; and deprived of government support, English education was kept up thereafter mainly by private enterprise.

The missionary societies, however, made up to some extent for the neglect of Government. The Evangelical Movement in England resulted in the establishment of a number of Christian missions in Ceylon. The Baptist Mission started work in 1812, the Wesleyan Missionary Society in 1814, and the Church Missionary Society in 1818. The Baptist and the Wesleyan Missionaries at first conducted schools in English, but after a short time they devoted their attention chiefly to Sinhalese schools in the villages like those run by Government. In this work they were followed by the Church Missionary Society and the American Mission, which began its work in Jaffna in 1816. From 1812 to 1832 the missionary societies opened 235 schools in which about 10,000 pupils were taught. These schools had a definite policy, were fairly well supervised, and their work unlike that of Government schools was carried on without interruption.

The Christian missions established a few English schools at their chief stations in order to train their workers. Those at

Kōttē and at Vaddukkoddai[1] gave a more advanced type of education like that given in an English secondary school today. The American Mission had a system by which an enterprising boy in a village could end his school career in the Vaddukkoddai school. And for the first time village lads began to benefit by the new learning, which in Government schools was enjoyed mainly by the Burghers and the children of headmen.

The Christian mission schools are no longer looked upon with the same favour. They are objected to on the ground that they have weakened the religious convictions of so many Buddhist and Hindu children. Some consider them the chief obstacle to the development of a system of state education which would satisfy the needs of all areas of the island. But had there been no Christian mission schools in the nineteenth century there would have been little learning in this island They certainly raised the moral and intellectual standard of their pupils, and prepared at least a small section of them for the changes that were taking place under British rule.

3. BUDDHISM AND HINDUISM

On the whole Buddhism and Hinduism suffered by the British conquest. In the Maritime Provinces they had lost the prestige which had attached to them as the religions of the rulers, and had entered into an unequal competition with Christianity. Before long they found themselves similarly placed in the Kandyan Provinces as well.

Buddhism and Hinduism had gone through a difficult time for centuries in the Maritime Provinces. The Portuguese had been hostile to them, and had destroyed the vihārēs and devālēs when waging war. The Dutch had not allowed the public worship of these religions and had almost compelled Buddhists and Hindus to become members of their Church. Buddhism had not fared well even in the Kandyan Kingdom. The constant wars had disturbed the life of the vihārēs, and the *Sangha* (the Buddhist Order) had deteriorated. The bhikshus had given up to a great extent their other-worldly form of life, and had begun to administer the vihārā lands themselves. There was a Buddhist revival in

1. The school at Kōttē is the present Christian College, and that at Vadduk-koddai is now Jaffna College.

the time of Kīrti Srī Rājasingha led by the saintly Välivita Saranankara, and the *upasampadā* (the ordination ceremony) was restored by Siamese bhikshus who were invited to Ceylon. But Buddhism was not restored to the position it had attained in the palmy days of Anurādhapura and Polonnaruva.

Buddhism had deteriorated also in other ways. Primitive Buddhism was distinguished not only by its emphasis on morality but also by its refusal to accept any religious claims based on birth. Buddha had proclaimed that one did not become a Brahmin by birth but by his deeds. But as time passed Buddhism itself had succumbed to the claims of birth, influenced by the theory of *karma*, Hindu ideas, and the 'feudal' society on which the Sangha depended for its maintenance. Quite early in the history of Buddhism bhikshus had begun to emphasise the status of the Buddha attained by his birth and traced his descent to the Solar dynasty of kings. In Ceylon later they had more or less accepted the caste system as the normal form of society for the laity. At this time in defiance of the rules laid down by the Buddha, they restricted the membership of the Sangha to the Goigama caste.

The British occupation led to no rise in the status of Buddhism. Protestant Christianity immediately received almost the same privileged position as it enjoyed under the Dutch as the religion of the rulers. Many Governors gave the Protestant Churches their direct support and preferred to appoint Christians to government posts.

Protestant Christianity had at this time another advantage over Buddhism and Hinduism. It did not merely substitute one dogma for another. It had shed much of the medieval and other-worldly character of Christianity, and no longer accepted society in the medieval way as a hierarchy ordered by God. It had been liberalized by Greek humanism and was being influenced by rationalist ideas which became popular during the eighteenth century. In other words Christian theology and organization had advanced with progress made in Europe, and was more suited to meet modern requirements than Buddhism and Hinduism which were still other-worldly in their outlook and organized in a form more suited to feudal conditions. Further the Christian ethic challenged the institution of caste, which many Ceylonese influenced by the new ways were soon to consider an obstacle to their advance.

Buddhism suffered on political grounds too. It has already been noted that British neutrality in matters of religion had not deterred North from helping to prevent the Sinhalese and the Tamils from returning to their old faiths. Maitland looked upon Buddhist bhikshus with suspicion. He tried to prevent them from obtaining their *upasampadā* at Kandy, the capital of the King, and to create rivalry among the bhikshus in the south in order to reduce their influence over the people.

The same political considerations made the British adopt a different policy in the Kandyan Provinces. In 1815 they did not wish to create any trouble for themselves by opposing Buddhism. They agreed by the Kandyan Convention to maintain and protect Buddhist rites, bhikshus and places of worship, and the Governor took upon himself the duties performed by the Kandyan King which gave him further political power. He appointed the Nāyaka Thēras and the officers in charge of the Daladā Māligāva and the devālēs, and placed the shrine which contained the *daladā* and the jewels that belonged to it in the custody of the British Agent of Government. He enforced the services rendered at religious festivals by those who held Māligāva and dēvāla lands, and gave grants towards their expenses out of the revenue of royal villages. Even the Kandyan Rebellion did not make the British Government change its attitude towards Buddhism. It continued to protect it as before, and only allowed other religions to establish places of worship within the Kandyan territory.

But the reforms effected by the British in 1818 affected adversely both the land-owning vihārēs and devālēs. Buddhism was so interwoven with the Kandyan system of life that no general change could be effected without disturbing it. When the Nilamēs in charge of the dēvāla lands were deprived of their judicial powers, they found it difficult to exact the services due from their tenants. The bhikshus who looked after vihāra properties found themselves similarly placed. If a tenant refused to perform his duty in the days of the Kandyan Kings, the bhikshus had only to appeal to the chief of the district to get the tenant punished. Now he had to take action in a court of law, a procedure to which he was not accustomed, and when he did so was often obliged to prove his title to his office. Even if he went through this process, it took some time before he obtained redress.

All the odds, however, were not against Buddhism. At the beginning of British rule there were 342,000 Protestant Christians. Most of them were Christians only in name, and with the neglect of the schools and the grant of religious toleration they began to return to their old faith.

In 1802 a *sāmanēra* (novice) of the Salāgama caste, Ambagahapitiyē, defying the Kandyan practice, went with five others to Burma and got themselves admitted to the Sangha. On their return they formed the Amarapura sect and threw it open to persons of all castes. It was unfortunate that this division in the Sangha arose owing to considerations of caste. Though the step taken by Ambagahapitiyē was the beginning of a movement to return to the original principles of Buddhism, under the circumstances caste prejudices did not cease to influence the activities of the bhikshus.

But these innovators could not bring Buddhism into line with the other changes that were taking place. The bhikshus in early times had been the leaders of light and learning. They had kept in touch with the developments in life and thought in India, assimilated new ideas, and helped Buddhism in Ceylon to flourish by adapting its forms of expression to changing conditions. But the Sangha, ignorant of English, held aloof from the changes now taking place. They withdrew to their vihārēs, studied the ancient books, went round the village for alms, and preached to the people. Thus they remained generally ignorant of the new movements and currents of thought that penetrated into Ceylon from the West.

4. RAJAKĀRIYA

Rājakāriya in Ceylon involved the performance of two classes of duties: unpaid services rendered by people for the repair and maintenance of the paths and bridges in their district, and services performed in respect of lands held and varying according to the caste of persons who performed them. A caste consisted of an exclusive social group, and the individuals that belonged to it did not as a rule eat with people outside the caste-group or marry outside it. No one could change his caste as it was determined by birth, and the caste to which a man or woman was born was held to be dependent on the merit earned by him or her in previous births. Certain castes were considered high and others low according to the occupation with which each was associated, and people of the so-called high castes considered it degrading to perform the work done by people of the so-called low castes. In short, caste consisted of a complete system of life and work in which every man knew his place, had regular work, and rarely exchanged it for another

The Portuguese and the Dutch governments had accepted this social system. The British Government too did the same at first in order to get its work done, and exacted the services due from each man according to his caste For instance, it demanded from one caste of people work as peelers, coolies, guards, and messengers of the Cinnamon Department. This work often involved great hardship but it had to be performed by everyone in the caste-group, each according to the sub-division to which he belonged. Anyone who failed to do his part of the work was given corporal punishment. In the same way services were exacted from persons of other castes according to their particular occupation.

A modern government like that of the British could not tolerate for long the two forms of *rājakāriya.* It did not agree with British ideas of justice, and serfdom was obsolete in England and condemned as a form of slavery. The British had arrived at a stage of society which was commercial and industrial, and *rājakāriya* hindered the progress of trade and industry by keeping the people bound to their occupations. In Ceylon its abolition was urgently necessary. It gave excessive powers to the chiefs and helped them to oppress their subjects, and as long as it prevailed the British were not able to get a secure hold over Ceylon.

North opposed *rājakāriya* on other grounds too. He was a man influenced more by theories than by hard facts. He believed that if the personal services by which lands were held were abolished and the lands given outright, the holdings would be improved and the country would grow in prosperity. Furthermore these results would lead to a rise in revenue. He ignored the fact that the people desired no such change and that the Madras Government had failed to effect such a reform. In 1802, contrary to British policy of the time which aimed at preserving ancient institutions, he abolished both these forms of *rājakāriya*, and ordered the people to pay as tax a share of the produce of all lands for which services were hitherto rendered.

North's changes, however, were not welcomed. The amount of labour performed for each holding had been fixed and generally was not heavy. Now instead a landholder had to give a share of the produce to Government. They had to pay more if they extended the cultivated area. The collection of the taxes was farmed out, and the farmer could harass them if he desired. Moreover they did not altogether escape the services as the chiefs continued to exact them. And their land could now be seized for debt as it was their personal property, while earlier a creditor had only a right to their crops.

Government too discovered that the change was not to its advantage. Many people showed unwillingness to work though they were offered payment, and North, though he retained the right to exact services in return for wages, consequently found it difficult to carry on the administration. During the war of 1803 he could not obtain the necessary labourers and had to recruit a corps from South India. Watchmen who did police duty in return for lands they held ceased to do their work, and crime increased in the villages.

Maitland did not approve of North's reforms. He did not interfere with the grain-tax substituted for services, but restored the fortnight's services rendered free for which North had agreed to pay. Brownrigg had to deal with the same problem in the Kandyan Provinces, and finally solved it after the Kandyan Rebellion in the same way as it was done in the Maritime Provinces. He abolished the services rendered for lands held and substituted a grain-tax retaining the right to exact the services, if necessary, either for wages or for exemption from the grain-tax. The fortnight's unpaid services was continued as before. The tenants in the *vihāragam*, the *dēvālagam*, and the *nindagam* were not brought within the scope of this law and could not look to the privilege of commuting the services they owed their lords. But the lords of such villages were within its scope as regards what they owed to the Crown and many a lord of *nindagam* who failed to pay his dues lost his *nindagam* and with it the services of his tenants.

5. AGRICULTURE AND TRADE

European rulers following the mercantilist ideas of this time promoted the development of the resources of their states in order to increase their revenue, and the British made it their policy to help the development of agriculture in Ceylon. This was not a new feature in Ceylon. Sinhalese kings who ruled at Anurādhapura and Polonnaruva had constructed large irrigation works to help the peasants to extend paddy-cultivation. They had taken advantage of the natural features to collect water by means of dams built across valleys or in the beds of rivers, from which it was conducted by means of channels to the fields below. The Dutch had kept some of these works in repair. The British found that the grain-tax was one of the chief sources of revenue, but yet large stocks of rice had to be imported, especially in time of famine. Therefore they made it their aim to make Ceylon self-sufficient as far as rice was concerned, and began to repair some of the large irrigation works.

The British also tried to introduce new crops and improved methods of cultivation. During the eighteenth century the Dutch and the British had vastly improved their methods of agriculture in Europe. By the application of capital to land they had introduced the rotation of crops to get the best results from the soil. In Ceylon too the British tried to make the people follow similar methods, and the Botanic Gardens introduced new field crops like the potato, turnips and Indian corn. They encouraged the transplantation of rice, and tried to make the people cultivate better kinds of rice like *mutusamba*. But they met with little success. The larger landowners did not undertake cultivation themselves but let out the fields for a share of the produce ; the peasants had neither the knowledge nor the capital to venture on new enterprises ; and Government, therefore, limited its activities to the supply of seed-paddy and agricultural implements.

The British followed the Dutch in other ways too. The Dutch East India Company had introduced commercial crops like coffee, cotton and sugar. It had helped the opening of plantations for the cultivation of these products. It had developed cinnamon plantations in places like Colombo the present Cinnamon Gardens and Kadirāna and other places, and worked them by *rājakāriya*. They had depended earlier on the cinnamon that grew wild in the low-country and the Kandyan Kingdom. But when the Kandyan rulers placed obstacles in their way, they had decided to have their own plantations in order to be independent of the supplies from the Kandyan Kingdom. The British developed still further the main cinnamon plantations. They tried to make the people open plantations and cultivate other crops. Here too they met with little success. The Sinhalese had neither the capital nor the educational attainments to take to such large enterprises, while the Europeans, under regulations that had been imposed by the East India Company, could not occupy lands outside Colombo.

Anxious to develop British commerce and increase the revenue of Government, Maitland removed this restriction on the Europeans. As a result many of them opened plantations of coffee, cotton, sugar, indigo and opium. Those who planted coffee found that in the Maritime Provinces it did not yield good results, and that it was not easy to compete with Ceylonese who produced it more cheaply. After the conquest of the Kandyan Kingdom the hill-country was found more suitable for coffee, and in 1823 George Bird opened the first European coffee plantation at Sinhapitiya near Gampola. Barnes took a keen interest in the cultivation of coffee and started a plantation of his own. He also established a government plantation at Gannoruva, where the Experiment Station of the Agricultural Department stands today Following his example, some of the Government Agents opened plantations in their own areas. The government plantations were worked by *rājakāriya* and the private ones with local labour. Local labour was not always available and in 1828 Barnes and Bird recruited 150 labourers from South India, but almost all of them deserted within a year.

Barnes did everything possible to encourage the cultivation of commercial crops. In 1825 he abolished the export duty on coffee and cotton. In 1829 he waived the land-tax for twelve years from coffee, cotton, sugar, indigo, and opium plantations. He exempted labourers employed in plantations from *rājakāriya* so that they might be able to work without interruption. These attempts undoubtedly encouraged the development of plantations. But the coffee planters of the highlands found that the transport of coffee by porters to the seaports was too expensive, and some of them abandoned the plantations they had opened. The situation changed considerably with the completion of the road to Kandy In 1832 a bullock cart carried 1,200 lb. of coffee for £1, whereas earlier the transport of an equal load required 30 porters who were paid £11 15s.

The valuable cinnamon trade of the island was taken over by the East India Company after the British conquest of the Maritime Provinces. When Ceylon became a Crown Colony, Government took over the cultivation and collection of cinnamon, and allowed the Company the monopoly of the trade. In 1821 the Government ceased to renew the contract to supply cinnamon to the East India Company, and took upon itself the exclusive right to sell cinnamon in Ceylon. In other words the cinnamon trade became a government monopoly once more.

Another product that was widely cultivated in Ceylon at this time was coconuts. There were according to Bertolacci's[1] estimate about 10,000,000 trees, and if 100 trees were allowed to an acre the area cultivated was about 100,000 acres. Coconuts were not cultivated on a plantation basis, the people being usually paid for the work of planting with a share of the trees. The coconuts and the products of the tree such as oi , copra, coir and jaggery were partly consumed in Ceylon ; the rest was exported mainly to the Coromandel Coast.

But the attempts to help the development of agriculture during this period did not have any far-reaching results, and the government expenditure continued to exceed its revenue.

Anthony Bertolacci was a Corsican who served in the Ceylon Civil Service from 1798 to 1819. His book, *A View of the Agricultural, Commercial and Financial Interests of Ceylon*, is the only work written on the economics or the economic history of Ceylon during the early British Period.

CHAPTER V

THE COLEBROOKE COMMISSION AND THE REFORMS OF 1832-33

1. THE COMMISSION

The Imperial Government, finding that the expenditure of the Ceylon Government exceeded its revenue year after year, sent W. M. G. Colebrooke in 1829 to examine the system of administration and C. H. Cameron in 1830 to report on judicial matters.

As a result of the Industrial Revolution Britain had become the workshop of the world, and consequently its economic, social and political organization had begun to alter. At the same time a powerful humanitarian current in the spiritual life of the British people had produced in them a deep sense of duty and a concern for the lot of the common people. These factors had in turn led to changes in ideas and values which were given expression to by writers like Adam Smith, Jeremy Bentham, James Mill and religious leaders like William Wilberforce. The basic doctrines of mercantilism, came under severe criticism, as well as certain of its characteristic features such as economic activities carried on by the State and monopolies which were avowedly set up for the common good but in actual practice benefited only a few. Privileges based on birth or ancient usage were opposed and equality of all men before the law was advocated. Utility became the chief objective in the assessment of things, and the greatest good of the greatest number, it was considered, should be the chief motive of government action. As a result of these ideas democracy was proclaimed the best form of government. At the same time individual rights were emphasized. Toleration and free discussion was welcomed, and freedom of thought, speech and action was advocated.

These ideas gradually gained ascendancy and by about 1820 began to dominate British politics. Monopolies and exclusive privileges were rapidly abolished. Archaic regulations which had no relation to the conditions or the ideas of the day were swept away. The legal system was reformed. Legal procedure was simplified and costs and delays in litigation were reduced. Autocratic forms of government were condemned and Parliamentary reform advocated. The opposition to slavery heightened and the interest in backward peoples increased.

It was when these ideas had begun to influence British colonial policy that Colebrooke and Cameron arrived in Ceylon. Their task was not limited to proposals for balancing the budget. They were instructed to inquire into the state of the Colony, its whole civil government, the state of its laws and the practical administration of justice. They were not required as in 1802 to maintain a strong government by keeping the powers of the Governor undiminished, to preserve the ancient institutions of the people, or follow Indian practice. On the other hand they were expected to recommend for Ceylon a system of administration in accordance with British conceptions of government.

With their disregard for tradition, their acceptance of utility as the criterion for assessing the value of things, their beliefs in private enterprise and free trade, in democracy and in the applicability of British institutions to all countries irrespective of their stage of development or differences due to their geographical and cultural environments, Colebrooke and Cameron could not appreciate the existing system of government in Ceylon, its general spirit or tendencies. They, therefore, began to make proposals to alter radically the entire system of government and the economy which it upheld in order to bring them into line with their own ideas.

2. THE ABOLITION OF RĀJAKĀRIYA AND OF MONOPOLIES

One of the first things that Colebrooke disapproved of was the medieval system of *rājakāriya*, even in the modified form it had assumed under the British Governors who had objected to it. The objections raised by North to these feudal services have already been mentioned. Colebrooke opposed them on both economic and humanitarian grounds. They hindered the development of agriculture and commerce by their interference with normal occupations. They denied the people the chance of changing their form of work or migrating from the district in which they lived. They reduced the people to a state of serfdom, and compelled Government to preserve distinctions of race and caste in order to get its work done and to deny equal rights to all its subjects.

Colebrooke raised objections also to the way *rājakāriya* was enforced. He found that the work did not fall equally on all people. A holding had to provide a male member for government work, but the holdings were not of the same size, not equally productive, nor owned by an equal number of persons. If a holding was owned by one man, he had to work for Government, and during that time neglect his own lands. Further the chiefs exempted to such an extent those who bribed them that the work at times fell very heavily on the others.

Colebrooke realized too that the attitude of most people toward *rājakāriya* was no longer what it had been in the days of North, and many now desired its abolition. It is possible that the administrative changes since the British occupation had undermined the relations that existed in the feudal economy and had begun to transform the outlook of the people. But what they mainly objected to was *rājakāriya* as exacted by the British. They were often employed outside their districts without adequate compensation The work they rendered before to government in clearing and maintaining village paths was light and directly beneficial to them, whereas work on modern roads and buildings was very heavy and was of no direct value to them as their economic conditions were primitive.

The Ceylon Government did not approve of a sudden abolition of *rājakāriya*. It did not want its work disorganized as in the days of North. But its arguments did not carry weight with the Imperial Government, and *rājakāriya* was abolished in 1832. The abolition of *rājakāriya* was opposed also by the chiefs and the bhikshus of the Kandyan Provinces. The influence of the chiefs depended on the continuance of the tenurial services and of the caste system. The bhikshus feared that the abolition would ruin the vihārēs and the devālēs that depended on the services of the tenants. Therefore the service tenures in the *nindagam*, *devālagam* and *vihāragam* were permitted to remain, and they continued to exist till 1870 when services were allowed to be commuted for payment.

The objections raised against *rājakāriya* applied equally to monopolies and other government activities in agriculture and trade as they were all carried on by means of these services. Colebrooke further objected to monopolies as he was opposed to mercantilism. If *rājakāriya* had prevented the feudal basis of society from changing into a commercial one, mercantilism as followed by the Dutch and the early British governors had prevented the development of free trade and private enterprise. The monopoly of the trade with India had been taken away from the East India Company, which had survived the assaults made on it for over a century. So Colebrooke opposed all commercial enterprises by Government.

Cinnamon was the chief government monopoly at this time. Colebrooke objected not only to the monopoly, but also to the system of cinnamon production as well as to the organisation of the trade. A whole caste of people was compelled to cultivate and collect cinnamon for wages which did not amount to more than was earned by a labourer. According to the cinnamon laws all cinnamon plants, wherever they grew, belonged to Government, and anyone who destroyed a cinnamon plant could be severely punished. Therefore the lands on which plants grew wild near cinnamon plantations went down in value. The government monopoly prevented the people from taking a share in the production and sale of cinnamon. The profits derived by Government too were not as large as they might have been had the trade been in private hands On Colebrooke's recommendation the cinnamon monopoly was abolished in 1833, and the cinnamon laws were repealed. Other monopolies also were discontinued, and activities in agriculture and trade abandoned. The coffee and pepper plantations were sold and the export of coconut oil and plumbago were given up.

Colebrooke also did not approve of direct taxes as they led to government interference in agriculture and industry. He objected to the land-tax, and the export duties which hindered the development and sale of the products of Ceylon, but he recommended only their gradual abolition as Government could not afford to abandon immediately these important sources of revenue. He also suggested the imposition of an export duty on cinnamon as he feared that Government would suffer by a sudden loss of income.

Colebrooke believed that these changes would remove restrictions on trade, the free movement of labour, and the liberty to cultivate any description of produce. He also expected that they would encourage private enterprise and lead to the accumulation of capital in the hands of the people and the development of agriculture and trade.

The abolition of *rājakāriya* is a landmark in the history of Ceylon. It put an end to the legal sanction which Sinhalese feudalism and the caste system hitherto received. It enabled the termination of the Governor's Courts, and placed all people irrespective of caste on an equal footing in the sight of the law. And above all the abolition of *rājakāriya* and monopolies made possible the commercial age which the British Government was trying to usher in.

3. ADMINISTRATIVE AND JUDICIAL REFORMS

Colebrooke along with Cameron also made proposals to liberalize the system of administration. Opposed to all forms of absolute government. Colebrooke disapproved of the almost unlimited powers possessed by the Governor. There were two regulations to which he specially objected. One enabled the Governor to banish or imprison indefinitely without trial any person who acted as an enemy of Government, or endangered the peace of the country The other prevented the Courts from examining the legality of any such act of the Governor. On Colebrooke's recommendation both these were repealed, and the Governor could no longer act in an arbitrary manner. In other words the repeal of these regulations brought the Government of Ceylon within the rule of law.

Colebrooke recommended also the establishment of Executive and Legislative Councils, and these were constituted in 1833. The Governor was requested to deal with all administrative and financial matters in consultation with the Executive Council. Though he was given the power to overrule its decisions, he found it difficult henceforth to ignore the advice of his counsellors. Whenever he went against them, he had to justify his action to the Secretary of State.

The Legislative Council was created in order to ensure that a certain number of responsible persons with competent local knowledge would examine the regulations which the Governor proposed to make. It was to consist of nine officials and six nominated unofficials to be nominated from the principal merchants and landowners of the people of the country. The officials were to be composed of the five members of the Executive Council and four others besides the Governor. Hitherto all laws in Ceylon had been made by the rulers or at their command by their officers. But an important change now took place. It is true that the Governor and the officials were not made responsible for their actions to the Legislature, and the fact of there being a clear majority of officials in the Council rendered the unofficials powerless. But henceforth the officials had to pay some attention to unofficial opinion, and Ceylon realized the beginnings of representative government.

Colebrooke also made recommendations to develop a common administrative system for Ceylon. Though the Kandyan Provinces had received a government similar to that of the Maritime Provinces, they still remained an independent unit whose officials were responsible to the Governor alone. Colebrooke found that this separate government helped to uphold the influence of the chiefs sometimes against the interests of their subjects, and that it prevented the Kandyans from assimilating thé ways of the people of the low country who had come under modern influences. He considered a union of the two governments essential for the development of the country, and on his recommendation the Governor was deprived of his special powers and the Kandyan Provinces were brought in 1833 under the same system of administration as in the Maritime Provinces. By the abolition of *rājakāriya* the differences in administration between the Sinhalese and the Tamil provinces had already been eliminated. And now was completed the administrative unification of all the three areas of the island Colebrooke recommended further the assimilation of the various divisions of the population by the development of a common system of law which would put an end to the conflicting systems that existed in the different regions or among classes of people in the same place and which would gradually approximate to the principles of British law.

Cameron, in his report, recommended the establishment of a common system of judiciary. He condemned the civil courts which were under the Governor on the ground that their methods of procedure were unsatisfactory and the legal knowledge of the officials inadequate. The result was that in 1832 a uniform system of courts was established to cover the whole island. The separate civil jurisdiction exercised by the Supreme Court over the Europeans was terminated, and both Europeans and Ceylonese were brought under the same system of laws unless the Ceylonese preferred to be judged by their own customs. The control of the civil courts by the Governor was abolished, and the Supreme Court was empowered to deal with appeals from the civil courts in addition to its criminal jurisdiction. In 1833 District Courts were established in the chief towns, and they were allowed to exercise civil and limited criminal jurisdiction within their areas. As District Judges had no knowledge of the customs and the conditions of the country, assessors were appointed to assist them. Cameron recommended further the inclusion of Ceylonese in the judicial service. Thus the distinctions between Europeans and Ceylonese were abolished. The separation of the judiciary from the executive was completed, and the administrative unification of the island was extended to the judicial sphere.

These reforms had far-reaching results. The administrative unification of the island gradually led the people of Ceylon to be treated as if they belonged to one nation. The reforms in the judiciary gave people civil liberty. The principle of representative government established through the Legislative Council prepared the way for the gradual introduction of representative and responsible government based on democratic principles. So Colebrooke and Cameron did much to direct Ceylon's development on modern lines.

4. REDUCTIONS IN EXPENDITURE

Since Colebrooke came to Ceylon not merely to reform the Government but also to reduce its expenses, he had to bring the expenditure into line with the revenue, and he did this by reducing the number of provinces and by cutting down the expenses of the Civil Service. He found that the lowland districts of the Kandyan territory were more closely connected with the coastal, and he detached them and joined them to the Maritime Provinces thus reducing the number of provinces to five: the Northern, the Western, the Southern, the Eastern and the Central.[1] A Government Agent was placed in each of the principal towns of

1 The Northern Province consisted of the districts of Jaffna, Mannār, the Vanni, the Island of Delft, as well as Nuvarakalāviya (Anurādhapura District which now forms part of the North-Central Province). The Western Province consisted of the districts of Colombo and Kalutara as well as Chilaw, Puttalam and the Seven Kōralēs (which now form part of the North-Western Province), the Four and the Three Kōralēs, and Lower Bulatgama (which forms the northern half of the Sabaragamuva Province). The Southern Province consisted of the districts of Galle, Mātara, Tangalle, Hambantota, as well as Sabaragamuva proper, and the Vällavāya and Buttala divisions of Lower Ūva and Vellassa (which now form part of the Ūva Province). The Eastern Province consisted of the districts of Batticaloa and Trincomalee as well as Tamankaduva (of the North-Central Province) and Bintänna (of Ūva). The Central Province consisted of the districts of Mātalē, Kandy, Yatinuvara, Udunuvara, Hārispattuva, Tumpanē, Dumbara, Hēvāhäta, Kotmalē, Upper Bulatgama, Uda Palāta and Valapanē as well as Viyalūva and Udukinda and Yatikinda (of Upper Ūva).

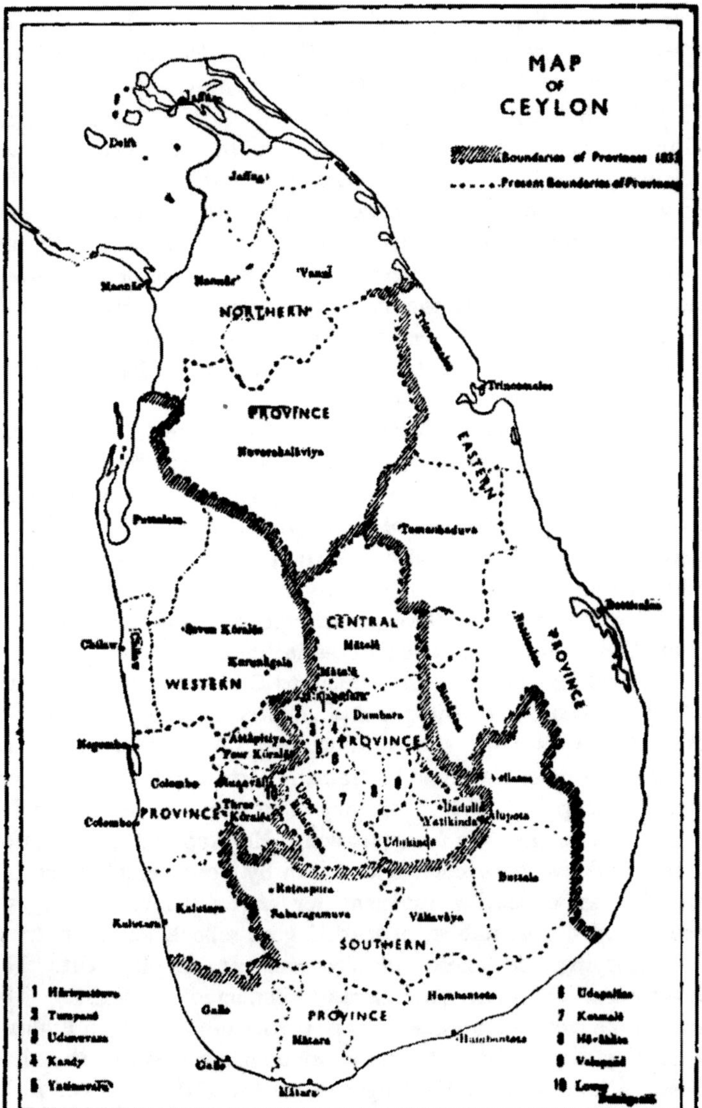
MAP
OF
CEYLON
Boundaries of Provinces 1832
Present Boundaries of Provinces
Delft
Jaffna
Mannar
NORTHERN
PROVINCE
Trincomalee
EASTERN
PROVINCE
Tamankaduva
Puttalam
Chilaw
CENTRAL
Mātalē
Kurunegala
WESTERN
Dumbara
PROVINCE
Four Kōralēs
Negombo
Colombo
PROVINCE
Colombo
Badulla
Uduhinda
Ratnapura
Sabaragamuva
Kalutara
Kalutara
SOUTHERN
Hambantota
Galle
PROVINCE
Mātara
Galle
Mātara
Hambantota
1 Hārispattuva
2 Tumpanē
3 Udunuvara
4 Kandy
5 Yatinuvara
7 Kotmalē
9 Valapanē

Jaffna, Colombo, Galle, Trincomalee and Kandy, and Assistant Agencies were established at Chilaw, Negombo, Kalutara, Kurunāgala, Ruanvälla, and Attāpitiya (Fort King) in the Western Province, Mannār in the Northern Province, Batticaloa in the Eastern Province, Matāra, Hambantota, Ratnapura and Alupota in the Southern Province, and Madavalatänna (Galagedara), Mātalē and Badulla in the Central Province. Colebrooke made even more drastic proposals affecting the Civil Service, and they were carried out in 1833. Pensions were abolished. Several of the higher posts were done away with, and sweeping reductions were made in salaries. Government further retained the right to fill the higher posts direct from England, and the Service was thrown open to all Ceylonese irrespective of caste, removing the distinctions that existed between the Europeans and the Ceylonese and opening all careers to talent.

Colebrooke was probably influenced by certain important considerations. In England at this time the Civil Service played a far less important part than in Ceylon, and he probably expected that with the abolition of *rājakāriya* and the government monopolies, and the gradual substitution of indirect taxes for direct ones, the separation of the judiciary from the executive and the establishment of a Legislative Council, the work and the importance of the Civil Service would be reduced in this country too.

In making these drastic reductions Colebrooke was no doubt influenced also by the view that a country like Ceylon could not afford to pay a large staff of European Civil Servants, and he hoped that Ceylonese would be trained before long to fill the higher government posts. With this object in view he recommended an increase on the vote for education. He proposed the abolition of the inefficient vernacular schools run by Government which did not give an education sufficient for contemporary needs, and recommended the establishment of English schools for the purpose of qualifying Ceylonese for government employment. The Government of Ceylon was already conducted in English. The work of the law-courts was soon to be carried out entirely in English. If the Ceylonese were to be usefu government servants, they had to gain a knowledge of the language, modes of thought, and ideas of their masters. He probably held the view that the government money could be more usefully spent in giving an English education first of all to the upper and the middle classes.

Colebrooke was also influenced in his proposal to establish English schools by the view held by Englishmen at this time that oriental learning was of little value, and that a knowledge of English would lead to the intellectual and moral improvement of eastern peoples. He probably believed further that a knowledge of English was a necessity if Ceylon was to emerge successfully from a feudal into a commercial society.

The proposal to abandon the vernacular schools and establish English schools may be criticized on various grounds. The change of the medium of instruction cannot be justified either by the lessons of experience or the findings of psychologists. But at this time Englishmen had far more faith in human nature and in the ability of human beings to change. They believed that if only the minds of people were filled with the right kind of knowledge, they would quickly transform themselves. The change was made not only in Ceylon but also in India, and under the conditions that prevailed no other step was possible. Colebrooke also appears to have acted unwisely in leaving English schools in the hands of a Commission consisting of Anglican clergy and government officials in a country where the majority of the people were non-Christian. But he could hardly have recommended for Ceylon a scheme in advance of England, whose education was still in the hands of the Churches. Besides there was no other body in Ceylon at the time that could have undertaken the work.

Whatever were the defects of these two proposals no one can condemn the spirit in which they were made. Colebrooke and Cameron believed that the bond between Britain and Ceylon could be maintained not by retaining British ascendancy in Government but by sharing power with the people by giving them offices of trust, maintaining friendly relations between Europeans and Ceylonese, imparting justice equally to all both rich and poor and by governing solely for the welfare of the people of thi Island. And had their recommendations been carried out fully, Ceylon would have been governed far more for the benefit of the people of the country than it was during the rest of the century.

PART II

FROM AN AGRARIAN TO A COMMERCIAL ECONOMY

CHAPTER VI

THE RISE OF THE PLANTATIONS AND THE SUBMERGENCE OF THE PEOPLE (1833-1850)

1. PLANTATIONS, TRADE AND LABOUR

The chief feature of this period is the growth of coffee plantations which gradually brought about a revolution in the economic conditions of the country.

The cinnamon trade, which was the chief source of revenue in Portuguese and Dutch times, ceased to be of importance by the end of this period. Till 1835 the British too derived considerable profit by the sale of cinnamon, but from that year its price began to fall owing to the competition of cassia and Javanese cinnamon. Cassia possessed a much coarser flavour, but was used because of its very low price. The cinnamon from Java was of the same quality as Ceylon cinnamon. The Portuguese and the Dutch were able to derive such large profits because Ceylon cinnamon was superior to all others. The Dutch, who had been deprived of this source of profit by the British, carried away from Ceylon in 1825 in one of their ships 3,000 cinnamon plants and seeds as well as a number of cinnamon peelers. Before long they sold cinnamon at a lower rate than Ceylon and began to capture the market. The Ceylon Government should have immediately reduced the export duty to enable Ceylon to compete with Java, but it took no such step as it did not want to lose its revenue. Even when it did reduce the duty, it did not lower it sufficiently to keep pace with the decreasing price. Finally the duty was abolished in 1853, but it was then too late to recover the trade in cinnamon.

The other agricultural products did not suffer in the same way. But there was no immediate expansion in their cultivation though according to Colebrooke's recommendations crown lands were sold at a nominal rate and were given free of land-tax and most of the obstacles that stood in the way of the development of agriculture and trade had been removed. Coffee had shown promise. The highlands had been found specially suitable for its cultivation, and the Colombo-Kandy Road had reduced the cost of transport to a twelfth. But many did not take to its cultivation either The Ceylon planters found it difficult to make much profit as they had to complete with the more experienced planters of the West Indies, and had to pay higher import duty in England on Ceylon coffee.

The situation began to change from 1837. In 1835 the English duty on Ceylon coffee had been reduced to the same level as that on West Indian coffee. At the same time the demand for coffee in Europe had increased and the supply from the West Indies (which went mainly to England) had declined owing to the liberation of the West Indian slaves. When the prospects of Ceylon coffee had begun to improve in this manner, R. B. Tytler, who had studied coffee planting in Jamaica for three years, arrived in Ceylon in 1837 and showed how coffee planting could be made more profitable by adopting the correct methods of cultivation.

The cultivation of coffee expanded immediately. In 1834 Government sold only 49 acres of crown land: in 1841 the sales went up to 78,685 acres, and in 1845 there were 35,596 acres under cultivation. The average annual export from 1828 to 1835 was 20,911 cwt. which was valued at £24,862. Even in 1837 the exports did not exceed 30,000 cwt. From that year cultivation steadily increased till in 1845 the exports rose to nearly 200,000 cwt. In 1835 there were only a few European planters in Ceylon: in 1848 there were 367 plantations with 60,000 acres under cultivation. The capital invested in coffee between 1837 and 1845 amounted to about £3,000,000.

The prospects of coffee appeared so bright that the Governor, Stewart Mackenzie (1837-1841), the judges, the officers of the army, and about half the Civil Servants all rushed to open plantations. They were joined by capitalists from India and England, and some of them bought existing plantations at exorbitant rates. But in their eagerness to acquire wealth they brought their own ruin. They were in such haste that they did not pay enough attention to the choice of soil and the methods of cultivation, and produced far less than they expected. The demand for labourers so exceeded the supply that in some cases the cost of labour even quadrupled. The department of the Civil Engineer and Surveyor-General could not keep pace with the demand for surveying lands and making roads. And the cost of transport by porters raised the cost of production still further. In 1844 the Imperial Government with its free-trade policy made matters worse by enabling coffee from Java and Brazil produced at a much lower cost to enter the market. It reduced the import duties on the coffee of these countries to the same level as on that of Ceylon. In addition to these drawbacks there were in 1845 and 1846 financial difficulties in Britain, and Ceylon planters could hardly obtain any credit. The result of all this was that most of those who invested money in coffee lost heavily, and the monetary crisis of 1847 in Britain paralyzed the industry for three years.

The spread of the plantations led to far-reaching economic changes. Not the least of these was the development of trade. When the British occupied the Maritime Provinces, the trade within Ceylon was of little consequence and its effects were not felt more than a few miles outside of Colombo. Even the foreign trade was not large and in 1825 amounted only to £521,000, though the British aimed at developing their trade by making Ceylon a market for British goods. It is true that the construction of roads broke down to some extent the isolation of the self-contained villages. The abolition of *rājakāriya* loosened the bonds which held together the ancient co-operative feudalism with its system of caste; and the abolition of monopolies, especially that of cinnamon, gave scope for private enterprise. These undoubtedly made trade possible, but it was the spread of coffee cultivation that gave the real impetus to the development of commerce. The peasants cultivated the fields to obtain food for their consumption and depended little on the world outside their village. On the other hand the large plantations did not produce food for local consumption but foi foreign trade. Their products were sent to the seaports to be shipped to other countries, while the food and other requirements of their workers were obtained from other parts of Ceylon or from abroad. This led to the growth of commerce within the island as with foreign countries, and the foreign trade of Ceylon in 1840 rose to £1,143,000, more than double that of 1825.

The trade of Ceylon would have expanded still further in the early years had there been banking facilities. There was no place for the deposit of money and no means of obtaining discounts or loans, and all banking operations had to be transacted through Madras or Bombay. But in 1841 a London merchant with foreign capital opened the Bank of Ceylon and in 1843 established a branch in Kandy, the centre of the planting districts. Government, in its desire to help the planting enterprise, supported the Bank. It was granted the right of limited liability which had been refused to the Ceylonese Agricultural Joint Stock Company the year before, and allowed to issue paper money without stamp duty, though it afforded no real security to the public. The Bank provided facilities for raising money in a manner unprecedented in Ceylon, and contributed no little to the expansion of the coffee industry as well as to its collapse at the end of this period. The Bank itself would have collapsed had not its business and liabilities been taken over in 1851 by the Oriental Bank of Bombay, which under its old name, the Western Bank of India, had established branches in 1842 in Colombo and Kandy.

The abolition of *rājakāriya* did not solve the labour problem on the plantations. Many expected that once people were released from their services to Government and were allowed to choose any occupations they desired, the plantations would get the labour they needed. But this did not happen. Every Sinhalese was attached to his village. Both by custom and according to Roman-Dutch Law he was entitled to a share of the property of his parents. When *rājakāriya* was abolished he tended his own lands, and did not show any desire to migrate from his village and work in the coffee plantations. Moreover if he was of 'high' caste, he considered it beneath his dignity to become a paid labourer. Thus the planters did not get enough labour to work their plantations. Sinhalese from the lowlands came and served as carpenters and masons. Villagers took part in destroying forests and opening up the land. But only a section of those who lived close to the plantations came for regular work as labourers.

The labour problem was finally solved as it had been in 1803 during the war against Kandy and in 1818 during the Ūva Rebellion. The labourers on the plantations were not employed on the same terms as feudal tenants. They received wages and not land as payment. They were in no way bound to serve their masters unless they entered into a contract of their own accord. In 1839 as many as 2,432 labourers came from South India. But this number proved insufficient. Besides even those who obtained an adequate number could not be certain of their labour force. They had to enter into contracts every year as the men returned to India after the coffee harvest. Even those contracts were often not honoured. The men often went to other estates which gave better treatment or offered higher rates of pay. The only remedy the planter had against these labourers was to take civil action, but the process through the law courts was slow and gave him little satisfaction. In 1841 Government, which had helped planters in other ways, passed an ordinance enabling an employer to take criminal action against an employee who broke his contract. However, conditions changed soon. There was more labour than was necessary, and the planters carried on their work without much difficulty.

Thus the plantations, though they contributed greatly to the prosperity of the country, were established mainly with foreign capital and worked mainly by foreign labour.

2. TRANSPORT AND COMMUNICATIONS

During this period Barnes' policy of building roads was continued, and the construction of steamships and the revival of the Mediterranean route established quicker communication between Ceylon and England.

Horton had not the same advantages as Barnes in the construction of roads. *Rājakāriya* could no longer be used, and on Colebrooke's recommendation the Military had been relieved of the work of making roads and bridges. But Horton continued the work through the Department of the Civil Engineer and Surveyor-General, reorganized in 1833, and before his departure in 1837 finished the task begun by Barnes of connecting all the provincial capitals of the island by means of roads.

Horton developed the road system in two directions. On the one hand he extended the arms of the old triangle north, north-east and north-west. In 1833 he extended the Colombo-Dambulla Road northwards to Jaffna and Point Pedro and north-eastwards to Kantalai, whither there was already a road from Trincomalee. A road was built to Anurādhapura from Arippu, the pearl-fishing centre, and another from Puttalam to Kurunāgala along the ancient trade route. On the other hand Horton constructed two important roads traversing the central highlands. He built the Kandy-Budulla Road which passed through Hāragama and Taldena across the Maha, Belihul, Kurundu and Umā Oyas, and completed the road from Kandy to Nuvara Eliya which had been traced as early as 1827. Thus Colombo was connected with Trincomalee, Point Pedro, Puttalam, Nuvara Eliya and Badulla, in addition to Galle, Mātara, Tangalla and Hambantota.

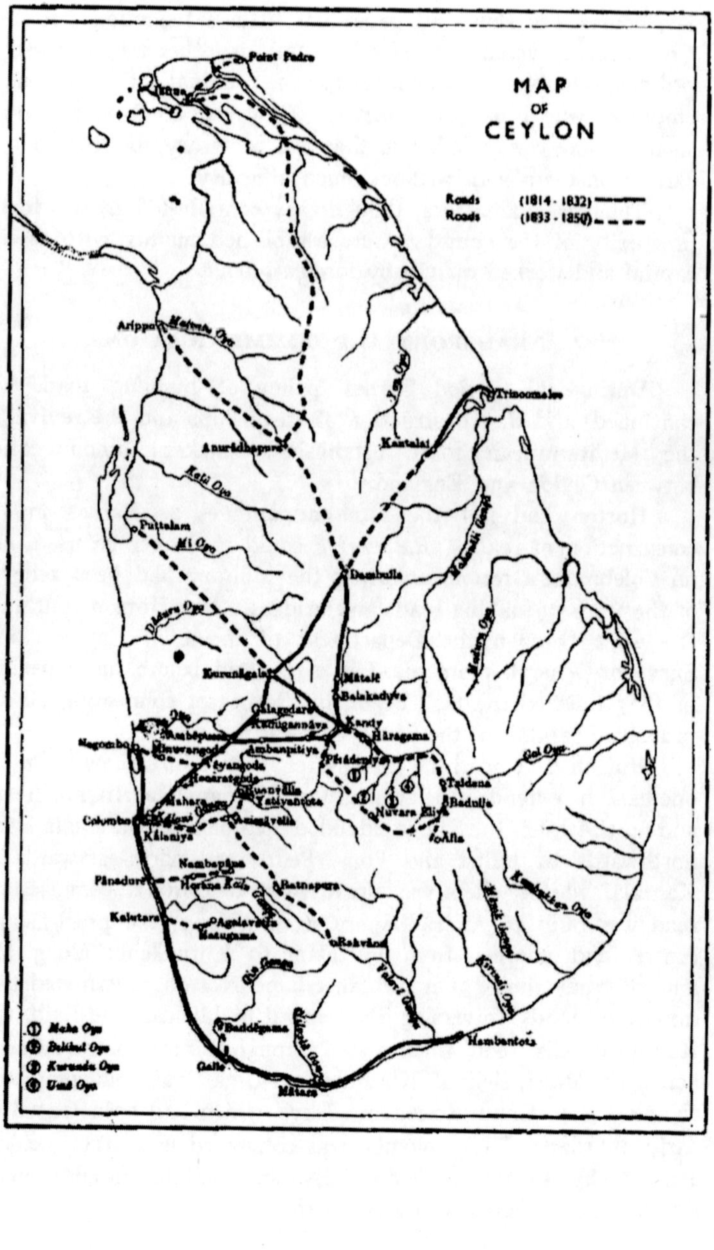
MAP
OF
CEYLON
Roads (1814 - 1832)
Roads (1833 - 1850)
Point Pedro
Arippo
Anurádhapura
Kantalai
Trincomalee
Kala Oya
Puttalam
Mi Oya
Dambulla
Mahaweli Ganga
Deduru Oya
Kurunágala
Mátalé
Madura Oya
Kandy
Háragama
Ambanpitiya
Negombo
Gal Oya
Taldena
Badulla
Nuvara Eliya
Colombo
Káłaniya
Nambapána
Pánaduré
Ratnapura
Kalutara
Agalavatta
Matugama
Kumbukkan Oya
Gin Ganga
Walawé Ganga
Kirindi Oya
Baddégama
Hambantota
Galle
Mátara
Maha Oya
Kurundu Oya
Umá Oya

The roads hitherto built were first for military and then for administrative purposes but after the departure of Horton the road policy of Government began to change. It has been pointed out that Government in order to increase its revenue had made special concessions in the time of Barnes to those who opened up plantations. For the same reason it now began in spite of its faith in the beneficent influence of individualism, to construct roads to help the planters to transport their produce. Since most of the high officials themselves had plantations, the early roads turned in the direction of their own estates, and the other planters expected that roads would soon be opened to assist them. But from 1837 to 1842 when planters needed roads most, the pearl fisheries failed and the Imperial Government imposed an annual payment of £24,000 towards the cost of the Ceylon garrison. So the Ceylon Government found that its revenue was insufficient not only to make new roads but even to maintain the existing ones.

The situation changed in 1843. The revenue of Government rose partly through the increased sale of crown lands, and the new roads it built and the old ones it restored from that year measured 1,247 miles. A road built from Colombo to Avissāvēlla and Ruanvälla along the valley of the Kalu Ganga following the ancient route to Kandy was continued to Yatiyantota, while another road was built from Avissāvēlla to Ratnapura ; this was extended to Rakvāna jointly by Government and a British company. The road from Colombo to Nuwara Eliy· was extended to Badulla, and then as far as Älla, whence there was a road-track to Hambantota through Vällavāya. A number of other roads were constructed from various points on the coast penetrating some twenty or thirty miles into the interior mainly to help plantations.[1]

Most of these roads are in the present Western and Sabaragamuva Provinces, and they helped to open up these areas. But many of the roads continued to be no more than paths where the forest was cleared, and the rest were only gravelled. A beginning

1 A road was built from Negombo to Vēyangoda, connecting Negombo with Kandy. Another was made from Negombo towards Kurunāgala as far as the sugar plantation of George Fraser, and a third from Pānadurē to Nambapāna gave access to a sugar plantation near Mahavak Oya which lay about 15 miles to the east of Horana. Two other roads were constructed, one from Kalutara to Agalavatta through Matugama, and the other from Galle to Baddēgama.

was made during this period to improve the roads themselves. In 1841 the Colombo-Kandy Road, and later a section of the road from Ambēpussa to Kurunägala, were metalled. This created another revolution in the matter of transport. A bullock cart, which hitherto needed thirty to forty days to make a return journey between Colombo and Kandy, now did it in six to eight days.

The construction of roads received another check in 1847 when the coffee crisis reduced the government revenue. Government now realized the importance of roads, and in order to keep up their construction went so far as to revive the old practice which had been abandoned in 1832. In 1848 Lord Torrington (1847-1850) passed the Road Ordinance which compelled every male inhabitant to give six days' labour to the building and repair of roads or pay a commutation tax of 3s.

The ancient Mediterranean route to the east had not been used after the Turkish conquests in the fifteenth century, and since then communications between England and India had been made by way of the Cape of Good Hope. But in the nineteenth century the route was revived with the use of steamships. The first steamships constantly needed fresh supplies of fuel and adjustments to their machinery and could not be used in open seas. They did not therefore replace the sailing vessels that took the Cape route, but plied in the land-locked Mediterranean and the Red Seas. Travellers from England went via Lisbon and Malta to Alexandria, from there to Suez by land, and again by ship to Aden and Bombay.

In 1841, the year in which the Colombo-Kandy Road was metalled, regular communication by sea was established between Galle and Bombay, and letters began to come to Ceylon monthly at first and then fortnightly. A reply to a letter from Galle to London by the Cape route took nine to twelve months, but by way of the Mediterranean the time taken was only about ten weeks.

From 1838 the letters that came to Galle were brought to Colombo by the mail coach which ran daily between the two towns. The *Colombo Observer* was not satisfied with its speed. In order to obtain without delay the despatches brought by the mail steamers, it established a pigeon service in 1850.

Thus the roads linked the various parts of the island with one another and helped the development of plantations and trade, while the steamships taking the Mediterranean route brought Ceylon into closer communication with Britain.

3. ADMINISTRATIVE CHANGES

While in most respects the recommendations of Colebrooke and Cameron were carried out, in the sphere of administration certain modifications were made. The drastic reforms made with regard to the Civil Service naturally led to much dissatisfaction in the Service, as they reduced the chances of promotion. Horton protested against these changes, and in 1836 he further pointed out that it was not satisfactory to recruit officers to the lowest class of the Service from Ceylon and appoint to the higher classes others from Britain who had no experience of the country. The Secretary of State thereupon began to fill some of the posts in that class with writers from Britain. This led to a demand for higher salaries and better conditions of service as the existing scales were insufficient to draw good men from Britain.

Besides, at the time Colebrooke arrived in Ceylon the Civil Service was far from efficient. Though Colebrooke suggested that the chief criterion that ought to guide promotion should be merit, this recommendation was not carried out. Since promotions generally came according to seniority, the officials neglected the study of Sinhalese and Tamil and made no special effort to improve themselves. Moreover many of them did not give their full time to their official duties. Though Civil Servants were not allowed to trade, they were not restricted from taking to agriculture. Encouraged by Government to open up plantations in order to increase its revenue, many of them availed themselves of the opportunity to add something to their meagre income, and devoted a considerable amount of time to their plantations.

Mackenzie's successor, Sir Colin Campbell (1841-1847), was unwilling to tolerate this state of affairs and pressed on the Secretary of State the necessity for further reforms. In response to his demand, Lord Stanley reformed the Civil Service in 1845. He ordered all Civil Servants to give up their plantations and devote their whole time to their official duties. He restored pensions, but in order to prevent officials from retiring early he ordered the payment of the pensions at fifty-five and not after twelve years of service as before. He compelled all Civil Servants to pass an entrance examination in England, and to qualify in Sinhalese or Tamil during their period of apprenticeship in Ceylon which had been re-introduced in 1838 by Mackenzie. He increased the number of posts in the Civil Service, and to ensure promotion put an end to appointments from outside the Service. At the same time in order to maintain the efficiency of the Service, he insisted that promotions should depend on merit and not on seniority.

In 1845 the number of provinces was increased to six. The division of Ceylon into five provinces proved economical as it led to a reduction of the number of Government Agents. The separation of the Kandyan lowlands from the highlands proved beneficial from the British point of view as it weakened the national strength of the Kandyans. But the arrangement reduced the efficiency of Government as the Government Agents could not from their stations supervise the outlying districts efficiently. For this reason in 1845 the districts of Chilaw and Puttalam together with the Seven Kōralēs, which once formed a part of the Kandyan Kingdom, were detached from the Western Province and constituted into the North-Western Province with Puttalam as its capital. The Assistant Agency at Kurunāgala was retained, but the one at Chilaw was abandoned and the district was administered from Puttalam.

The construction of roads led to other changes. A number of Assistant Agencies, which had been established mainly for military reasons, were abandoned.[1] New Assistant Agencies were established at Kāgalla on the Colombo-Kandy Road, at Nuvara Eliya on the Kandy-Badulla Road and at Anurādhapura on the Kandy-Jaffna Road. Roads also made Bintänna more easily accessible from Badulla, and Ratnapura from Colombo. Consequently in 1837 the district of Bintänna was detached from the Eastern Province and attached to the Badulla District of the Central Province, and in 1845 the Ratnapura District which formed part of the Southern Province was attached to the Western Province.

There was also a change in the judicial sphere. The establishment of the principle of equality in matters of law led gradually to the creation of a consciousness of positive rights among a small

1 Negombo, Kalutara, Ruanvälla and Fort King in the Western Province, Alupota in the Southern Province, and Mātalē and Madavalatänna (Galagedara) in the Central Province.

section of the people. Though Government treated all its subjects as possessing equal legal rights, the people who had enjoyed special privileges did not adjust themselves to the new situation at once, and the 'upper' section of the Goigama caste refused to sit on juries with members of their own community who belonged to the 'lower' section. This led to a controversy in which others also took part. In earlier times persons who belonged to each caste accepted its position in the social scale and hoped to improve their position only in the next life. In 1803 Ambagahapitiyē had refused to accept this position regarding the Sangha. The Sinhalese who were influenced by the study of English and the new economic conditions now refused to be treated as inferiors merely on the score of birth, and in 1843 all distinctions of caste and of their sub-divisions observed in the choice of jurors were abolished.

4. THE LEGISLATURE

The Legislature underwent little change during this period. The Council established in 1833 on Colebrooke's recommendation met for the first time with only the official members. Horton could not include unofficial members as no Sinhalese or Tamil, belonging to the commercial or agricultural classes, who had a sufficient knowledge of English to qualify him for nomination as a member of the Council was available. Finally he gave a Sinhalese and a Tamil who were government interpreters pensions equal to their salaries, and nominated them along with a Burgher in 1835. The other members could not be nominated till 1837 owing to the difficulty of finding suitable candidates among the British merchants, who were mere agents of foreign houses and had neither property nor any permanent or abiding interests in the country.

Under the influence of British radical thought there was a demand from the very beginning for a Legislative Council that contained more unofficial members and possessed the right to control the expenditure of Government. It was even suggested by a few European merchants and Burghers that the executive should be made responsible for its actions to the legislature; that election should replace nomination; and that the vote should be extended to uneducated Sinhalese and Tamils. The Europeans[1]

1 The word European is used as there were a few who were not British.

were dissatisfied with Government's progress in building roads. They hoped, if they succeeded in getting such a council, to be able to force the executive to carry out their wishes. The Burghers with their English education secured most of the clerical posts under Government, while the more able among them entered the legal profession. They believed that British institutions could be applied to other countries, and that self-government or some advance in this direction was a right they could claim as British subjects. Their opposition to Government was no doubt also due to other considerations. Though the Civil Service was opened to Ceylonese in 1833, its vacancies were almost solely filled by Europeans, and the appointment of Burghers to higher posts in the judiciary was opposed by them.

These demands were opposed by the Government of Ceylon. It contended that the people of Ceylon were fit only for a paternal form of government; and that if representative government were established, it would serve the interests of the European merchants who had no stake in the country and not those of the permanent inhabitants. The Imperial Government upheld these objections and refused to accede to the demands for a reformed legislature. But it made one small change. At this time the Government of Ceylon could not interfere with the fixed establishment charges such as the salaries paid to officials which were fixed or approved by the Secretary of State, but could apportion as it pleased what remained after these charges were paid. In 1840 the Imperial Government transferred to the Legislative Council the appropriation of this amount.

5. EDUCATION

Colebrooke's recommendations with regard to education prevailed almost to the end of this period. In 1832 the Government Sinhalese and Tamil schools were abolished, and five English schools were established in Colombo, Galle, Jaffna, Kandy and Chilaw. In 1836 the Colombo Academy (now called Royal College) was opened as a secondary school. It was expected to provide teachers for other schools. The number of English schools soon rose, and in 1848 there were sixty of them with an attendance of 2,714 pupils. They included three Central Schools in Colombo,

Kandy and Galle for boys,[1] three Superior Schools for girls, and sixteen girls' schools.

In 1832 the schools were entrusted to government chaplains and their management to the Archdeacon, the head of the Church of England in Ceylon. In 1834 according to Colebrooke's recommendation the first School Commission, similar in organization to the Board of Scholarchen of the Dutch, was appointed to supervise the work of the Government schools. This Commission functioned in Colombo and was assisted by committees in Galle, Jaffna, Kandy and Trincomalee, the provincial capitals. The Commission and the committees consisted of the clergy of the Church of England and government officials.

The School Commission did not prove a success. The quarrels and jealousies of the Christian sects, the Anglicans and the Nonconformists, which marred educational progress in England affected Ceylon too, and there were conflicts between the Anglican clergy who ran the Government schools and those of other Christian denominations. As a result the School Commission was replaced in 1841 by the Central School Commission in which the laity were in a majority. Its membership was widened by the inclusion of unofficial laymen and the clergy of other Protestant denominations and of the Roman Catholic Church.

In 1839 the distribution of the government grant for education in England, which hitherto had been entrusted to religious societies, was handed to a committee of the Privy Council. This committee tried to raise the standard of schools by giving grants according to recommendations made by inspectors who visited the schools. These changes were not without effect on Ceylon. The secretary of the new Commission was appointed Inspector of Schools, and superintendents were appointed to assist him in the work of inspection. Before long Government took further steps to improve the schools which were generally inefficient. The Central Schools for boys established in 1843 and 1844 were made to take up the training of teachers, and in 1846 a school for the training of teachers for Sinhalese schools was established at the request of the Christian Missions.

1 These were designed to give 'such an impetus to practical education that youths will take the opportunity to qualify themselves for agriculture and other lucrative employments'. But these objects were lost sight of before long.

All Government schools were really Anglican schools. Christian religious education was given in all of them, and though attendance at their classes was not compulsory, in actual practice no pupils kept away from them. In the Jaffna peninsula the mission English schools were run efficiently and Government owing to difficulties in administration left English education in their hands in 1842, and assisted them with grants. Government also gave aid to other English institutions which deserved support. In 1839 it gave a grant to the Roman Catholic Church to help the establishment of a Roman Catholic English school in Colombo.

The experience gained by the Commission during these years made it realize that English was not a satisfactory medium of instruction for Sinhalese and Tamil children, and before the end of this period arrangements were made for such children in English schools to begin their education in Sinhalese or Tamil. About the same time the Christian missions which carried on Sinhalese and Tamil schools found that they were unable to extend their work; and in 1847 the Commission, abandoning Colebrooke's recommendation, began to establish Sinhalese and Tamil schools. The Commission also realized that the education would not be fully effective until that of girls too was taken in hand, and began to remedy this defect. But educational expansion came to an end with the coffee crisis. Very soon drastic cuts were made in the education vote and many of the schools were abandoned.

Government's new educational policy based on Colebrooke's recommendations led to certain definite results. The centres of education moved from the villages to the towns. Those who benefited most by this step were the Burghers, who lived mainly in the urban areas, and had little provision hitherto for their education. Being for the most part Protestants, they had no religious scruples about attending these English schools and soon filled half the places in them. By means of the education they received, they obtained employment in the government service. Some of them turned to the practice of law, and took advantage of the new avenues of work opened by the legal and judicial reforms carried out on Cameron's recommendations. The other Protestants followed them in attending the Government schools, but few Roman Catholics did so. Their priests who came from Konkan in Western India did not know sufficient English to run English schools themselves. So the Roman Catholics appealed to the Pope, and it was the European priests he sent who established the English school in 1839.

The study of English though taken up by a small section of the people had far-reaching results, similar in many ways to the effects of the study of Greek in Europe in the fifteenth century. The Sinhalese and the Tamils had literatures of their own. They had also a classical literature in Pali and Sanskrit derived mainly from India. These works were mainly religious and a large proportion of them emphasized the other-worldly view of life. Though early Buddhist teaching was rationalist in some respects and permitted people to exericse their own judgment, later writings had accepted the 'medieval' social system with its emphasis on authority On the other hand, English presented its students with the progressive and liberalizing ideas of the civilization of Europe, and stirred by these they began to act in new ways instead of merely following their ancient customs and the ways of their elders. Through the medium of English they studied the arts and sciences of Europe and learn what was happening in other parts of the world. The study of English history made them acquainted with new institutions. They learnt how the British middle class gained control of the government in England, and as time passed they began to demand similar constitutional reforms in Ceylon.

An account of the educational activities of this period would be incomplete without a reference to the Press which was considered at this time a medium of diffusing knowledge. In the early days of British rule the only publication was the *Government Gazette*. It contained also foreign and local news and by the time Horton arrived this news section formed a separate supplement. At that time there was no considerable body of people who felt the want of a newspaper. The means of communication within the country and with other countries were unfavourable for its development, and the Governor's powers were such that no one could criticize Government with safety. But the situation changed with the development of roads, the abolition of the special powers of the Governor, and the other reforms brought about by the Colebrooke Commission.

Horton, who looked upon the newspaper as an educational agency—expanded the news supplement of the *Government Gazette* into the *Colombo Journal*, and invited the public to contribute articles expressing their opinions. This paper was stopped as the

Colonial Office did not approve of a government newspaper. Its place was then taken by *The Observer*, started in 1834 by the European merchants and changed into the *Colombo Observer*. From its very inception this weekly sheet advocated radical changes of all kinds and criticized Government unhesitatingly. A free press is hardly compatible with an autocratic form of government, but the Governor took no steps to curb it. The Liberal ideas that prevailed in England at this time were in favour of free expression of opinion. Even in India the press censorship was removed in 1835. Besides the critics were all Britishers, and though they wanted the form of government changed, they made no attempt to end British rule in Ceylon. All that the government officials did was to support the *Colombo Chronicle*, which was started in opposition to the *Observer*. The new paper changed its name into the *Herald* in 1838 and the *Ceylon Times* in 1846. In the same year some British merchants published another paper, the *Ceylon Examiner*. On the whole the Press took up the cause of the European merchants and planters whom they represented, and helped the unofficial members to press their claims on Government.

Printing presses were not owned only by the newspapers and Government. The Wesleyan Missionary Society and the Church Missionary Society established printing presses soon after they began work. During this period the Baptist Missionary Society set up a printing press at Kandy and the American Mission four presses in the North. These presses issued innumerable tracts, magazines, and books. The American Press began its weekly newspaper, the *Morning Star*, in 1841. These publications provided a considerable amount of reading matter to pupils who passed out of Mission schools, and together with the secular newspapers exercised a considerable influence over those who were literate.

6. BUDDHISM AND HINDUISM

Though Colebrooke did not approve of the connection of the Ceylon Government with Buddhism, he did not propose any important changes, and Government continued to extend its protection to Buddhist property in the Kandyan provinces. A share of the revenues of the *gabadāgam* went towards the celebration of certain Buddhist festivals. When the *gabadāgam* were sold after the abolition of *rājakāriya*, Horton arranged t make annual payments instead as he did not wish to break away from earlier declarations.

But during this period the Christian missionaries and their powerful friends in England, who believed that a British Government should associate with no other religion than Christianity, opposed Government's connection with Buddhism which they considered an idolatrous faith; and they were supported by the Secretary of State. The result was that Buddhist property, which had already suffered from the abolition of *rājakāriya*, began to be neglected with the severance of Government's connection with Buddhism.

The first to take steps in this direction was Mackenzie, who was carried away by his religious scruples. He refused to sign warrants which gave recognition to acts of appointment; and the bhikshus and the Nilamēs, deprived of their legal status, could neither safeguard the properties of the vihārēs and dēvālēs nor compel their tenants to render the services due from them. His action even affected the right of the bhikshus to be in charge of vihārēs, and of the tenants to occupy vihārē or dēvālē lands. A Disāva seized a vihārē and ejected its incumbent, but the bhikshu could obtain no redress in the courts as he had not been legally appointed. Mackenzie and his successor Campbell were thus compelled to sign warrants in some instances.

Campbell, the officials, and the members of the Legislative Council opposed the complete severance of Government from Buddhism. But in 1847 the Secretary of State compelled Torrington to abstain from making appointments of bhikshus and Nilamēs, to hand over the *daladā* to the Mahanāyaka Thēras and the Diyavadana Nilamē, and to grant crown lands yielding an annual income of £350 in place of the annual payment towards the cost of the Daladā Māligāva rites.

The problem was to find a substitute to take the place of Government. Campbell suggested the appointment of a committee of chiefs to take charge of the duties carried out by Government. But the Buddhist bhikshus, who had never been accustomed to any interference in their affairs by laymen especially regarding matters of internal discipline, disapproved of the proposal. The Secretary of State objected as it increased the power of the chiefs, and the proposals did not complete the act of severance between Government and Buddhism. He suggested that the

Buddhist bhikshus should take into their hands the management of Buddhist property. He probably did not realize that Buddhist bhikshus did not form an organized body like any Christian Church, and by their own rules were prevented from dealing with temporal affairs though at this time many bhikshus in Kandyan territory were managing vihārē properties.

Buddhism and Hinduism also suffered by the fact that they had not the men, the organization, or the funds like the Christian Missions to establish schools. Buddhist and Hindu children who wanted an education had to attend Protestant schools, which were run mainly with the object of converting Buddhists and Hindus to Christianity. It is true that a considerable number of Buddhist children still learned to read and write from Buddhist bhikshus, but the education imparted in the vihārēs was in Sinhalese, and not organized as in schools run by Government and the Missions. On the whole the influence of Buddhism and Hinduism appears to have waned during this period, and many Sinhalese and Tamils appear to have considered it more fashionable to call themselves Christians, whatever their actual beliefs were. It would be untrue to say that Christian workers met with no opposition at all from Buddhists and Hindus, but neither religion had an organization or the men to counteract the activities of the Missions.

7. THE PEASANTS AND THE DISTURBANCES OF 1848

'We profess to govern for the exclusive good of the natives of the country, and devote our attention almost exclusively to make the culture of the soil profitable to European adventurers'. So wrote James Steuart[1] in his *Account of the Pearl Fisheries* printed in 1843.

It has been shown how the proposals made by Colebrooke and Cameron led to the unification of the administration, the establishment of the Executive and the Legislative Councils, judicial and legal reform, the investment of British capital, the development of plantations and trade, the rise in revenue and the disappearance of the annual deficit, the development of the means of communication, and the growth of English education and the Press. But all these changes failed to benefit the peasants. As

1 James Steuart was Master Attendant of Colombo from 1825 to 1855 and was the founder of the firm of George Steuart and Company. His *Notes on Ceylon* is critical of Government.

time went on their institutions were submerged by the new forces at work and their condition deteriorated. Government, pressed by the unofficial European members of the Legislative Council and the newspapers, devoted its attention mainly to the needs of the European merchants and planters; and showed little concern for the peasants, who had no way of bringing their wants to the notice of the officials.

Earlier, Government had done much to improve peasant agriculture and irrigation. Commercial and agricultural interests then, as Bertolacci said, depended almost entirely upon the encouragement which Government afforded to the cultivation of rice. Conditions had changed since. Government now expected miracles from the investment of British capital in developing plantations, and devoted all its attention to secure facilities for planters. It ignored the recommendation of Colebrooke that part of the money received from the redemption of the grain-tax and the sale of waste land should go to the repair of ancient tanks and water-courses. It definitely neglected large tracts in the Dry Zone which had been under cultivation in earlier times, and only in one province did it attempt to increase the means of irrigation and to extend the cultivation of rice. In 1837 the dams at Kirama and Ūrubokka which irrigated one-third of the area between the mountains and the south-east coast were destroyed, but nothing was done to restore them. Earlier in 1833 Skinner reported that the population of the Anurādhapura District was rapidly decreasing owing to disease and drought, and that the state of the peasants was distressing to behold. At the time Government had not the money to attend to their needs, but it took no steps to relieve them even when its finances improved.

Conditions in Ūva, where irrigation works had been damaged during the Rebellion, were even worse according to a report submitted in 1855 to Ward by Bailey, the Assistant Agent of Badulla. The large canals were out of use and were traceable only by the remains of their vast embankments The six or seven large ones, which yet irrigated a considerable extent of land, were in a dilapidated condition and hastily and imperfectly patched up. The only stone dam known to him was in bad order. A masonry sluice was a thing unknown, and when cultivators wanted water they cut a hole in the bank wherever it suited them. Droughts and the destruction of the tanks had reduced the population, and the peasants who survived were poor, sickly, apathetic and too listless even to repair small village tanks.

The situation in the Dry Zone would have been better had Government maintained the gansabhāvas. From ancient times the gansabhāvas had regulated every detail of agriculture and assigned to each cultivator his particular share in the use and the preservation of the irrigation works. They punished those who did not perform their part of the work or violated the customs of the village. But now they had not the power to enforce their decisions. While the abolition of *rājakāriya* deprived them of the means by which they obtained the co-operation of the peasants, the establishment of the courts took away their power to punish those who disobeyed their orders. Without co-operation the peasants could not carry on their activities, and the only place to which they could go for the redress of their grievances was the law-courts, where the judges often gave wrong decisions in their ignorance of the minute and complicated details of rice-cultivation regulated by custom.

The new land laws cut at the root of the co-operative social life of the villagers. They made their lands alienable and their partition easy. The peasants themselves, influenced by the new forces which encouraged individualism, began to resort to litigation in the courts. The courts undoubtedly gave some protection to people, but they were presided over by European magistrates and conducted in English according to European forms of civil and criminal procedure with the aid of interpreters and lawyers. Such a system could not help villagers who had neither the means to employ professional lawyers nor the knowledge of the laws to make use of them to their advantage. Cases often went on for years without being settled, and while lawyers benefited the villagers were impoverished.

These disputes regarding property led further to a large number of petty criminal complaints, both true and false. There were charges and countercharges of cattle trespass, malicious injuries to fences and boundaries, thefts of fruit, assaults, threats, and trivial offences. These were usually the result of ill-feeling between the litigants arising out of previous differences, and the courts were used not so much to obtain redress for wrongs as to avenge petty social quarrels. Such disputes in earlier times were settled summarily on the spot by the gansabhāvas and were not allowed to be carried further. But now they led to much bitterness among the villagers and to a gradual deterioration of the standards of village life.

All these misfortunes of the villagers were not due to the recommendations of Colebrooke and Cameron. On the contrary some of the evils described were rather due to the neglect of some of their proposals. Colebrooke and Cameron did not recommend the introduction of British institutions regardless of the conditions that existed in Ceylon. Colebrooke realized that the people of the rural areas still needed a paternal form of government. He, therefore, recommended the revival of the regulation made by Maitland in 1808 which required the Collectors to make regular circuits through their districts and settle all petty disputes and so make it unnecessary for the villagers to go to a distant court for this purpose. Cameron suggested several modifications to adapt the new system of courts to local conditions. He recommended that the cases should be conducted in a way to suit the people and that every suitor who made false allegations should be punished to prevent vexatious legal proceedings. Colebrooke also wanted the ancient institution, the gansabhāva, continued and that it should be allowed to deal with petty cases. It is true that neither Colebrooke nor Cameron made detailed recommendations showing how an institution like the gansabhāva, which existed under pre-feudal conditions when government was personal, could be adapted to a modern bureaucratic form of government inspired by the beneficient influence of individualism which they envisaged. But that they could be adopted were shown when the Government revived them in the latter half of the nineteenth century to meet the very abuses which Cameron anticipated and showed ways of avoiding.

The expansion of the plantations, though it gave work to many villagers, was not welcomed by them. It is true that planters did not require the low-lying valleys where paddy was cultivated. But when there was no proper survey of lands before their sale, many villagers were deprived of their high lands where they carried on *chena* cultivation or grazed their cattle. Having depended for generations on land for their existence and being intensely attached to it, they probably looked with dismay upon the occupation of the areas around them by foreigners, and, resented the appropriation of any land already occupied by them.

The rapid development of the coffee industry in the forties helped further to unsettle conditions in villages in the plantation areas. The plantations offered many new forms of employment such as the work of contractors, transport agents, traders, carpenters, masons and tavern-keepers. The Kandyans, who had little education and less contact with foreign ways, refrained from following these new walks of life, and were exploited by some of the low-country people who flocked to take up these occupations. They suffered further by the spread of taverns in the estate areas. Government in its desire for revenue did not take any effective teps to check their increase, and they became responsible for a great deal of intemperance and vice which spread to villages.

The position of the peasants would not have degenerated in this manner had the Civil Service been efficient. Many of the Civil Servants who devoted much of their time to their plantations failed to tour their districts regularly, and neglected the study of Sinhalese and Tamil. The roads constructed outside the plantation areas were not kept in repair, and the closing of the Government Sinhalese and Tamil Schools did not make visits to villages as necessary as before. The Sinhalese chiefs who controlled the rural areas made no effort to acquaint the Civil Servants with the real conditions in the villages. The British had undermined their power, and the people were not submissive to them as before. They resented the treatment they received and took little interest in their work. The Civil Servants thus lost touch with the villages, and though Colebrooke recommended the preservation of the gansabhāvas, they took no steps to check their decay.

It was while the villager was in this discontented and unsettled state of mind that Government, partly to meet the deficit created by the coffee crisis, introduced new taxes. The stamp duty was increased. Owners of shops, boats, carriages and bullock carts were made to pay an annual licence fee of £1. An owner of a musket was ordered to pay 2*s*. 6*d*. and the owner of a dog 1*s*. Every male inhabitant was asked to work six days a year on the repair and construction of roads or pay a tax of 3*s*. The increased stamp duty affected those engaged in litigation. Almost every village home had a dog. The tax on guns affected the villager further as a gun was essential for protecting his crops. The road-tax was interpreted by him as a restoration of *rājakāriya* and he objected to it as no direct benefit accrued to him by the construction of roads.

On the 6th July, 1848, a crowd of about 4,000 people presented a petition against the taxes. Resentment against the imposition took shape in a series of disturbances in the Mātalē and the Kurunāgala districts, which according to Skinner were the worst governed areas of the island. Led by two low-country Sinhalese who were professional robbers, mobs sacked public buildings and shops at Kandy, Mātalē and Kurunāgala, as well as some planters' bungalows.

These riots can hardly be called a rebellion, but Government which was ignorant of the real conditions of the country misjudged the situation and took severe measures to put them down. It interpreted the disturbances to be a rebellion of Kandyan chiefs and bhikshus to overthrow British rule. The repressive measures taken by Torrington were strongly resented by a section of the educated classes, who made representations to the Secretary of State as well as to other members of Parliament. In response to them a Parliamentary inquiry was held by a Committee of the House of Commons. Lord Torrington was recalled and two other officials were dismissed. The licences for firearms, dogs and shops were repealed.

CHAPTER VII

THE DEVELOPMENT OF THE COUNTRY (1851-1872)

1. PLANTATIONS AND LABOUR

Coffee began to revive once more after the depression of 1847-1850. It recovered completely by 1853 and the output steadily increased till 1870. Coffee estates began to pay. They were now worked economically, and the price in London which had gone down to 27*s*. per cwt. had risen to 41*s*. in 1850. The exports in 1850 were 378,473 cwt. with a value of £609,263. In 1855 they rose to 506,540 cwt. with a value of £1,025,282, and in 1870 they amounted to 1,059,030 cwt. valued at £2,753,005.

With the recovery of coffee land sales rose. In 1857 European plantations under cultivation covered 80,950 acres. Within ten years the area occupied by them more than doubled. In 1857 Ceylonese owned about 48,000 acres of coffee, and between 1849 and 1869 from one-half to one-fourth of the total quantity of coffee exported was theirs. Their plantations were mainly in Hunnasgiriya, Mātalē East and the Badulla District. Besides these, almost every Ceylonese who owned a piece of land in the old Central Province grew some coffee.

The Ceylonese who took a share in the coffee enterprise as planters, merchants, transport agents and contractors earned a great deal, and gradually improved their standard of living. These changes, together with the spread of English education and the increased facilities for travel, gradually transformed their habits and their ideas. Ancient social values were undermined. Many who acquired wealth refused to accept any longer the restricted status given to them by their caste, and caste controversies became a feature even in the Sinhalese press.

Since the plantations depended to a great extent on immigrant labour, Government gave constant attention to the labour problem. In the early sixties there was a shortage of labour. South Indian labourers began to be drawn away to Mauritius and the West Indies where they were provided with higher wages and better medical facilities. Government met the situation in two ways. In 1857 Ward provided greater inducements for labourers to come to Ceylon when he feared that the plantations would suffer owing to the extra labour needed for building railways and roads. In 1861 Government arranged for four vessels to ply between the islands of Rāmēsvaram and Mannār to convey the labourers that came from India to Ceylon, and from 1866 gave a Bombay company an annual subsidy for three years to convey labourers regularly from Madras and Negapatam and intermediate ports to Colombo.

The second method Government adopted to attract labourers to Ceylon was to improve their conditions here. In 1861 it passed the Lengthened Engagements Ordinance which secured the rights of immigrant labourers and enabled employers to turn their work to the best account. In 1865 it made it compulsory for employers to provide medical aid to labourers. As the planters failed to established a satisfactory system, in 1872 Government at the request of the Secretary of State passed an ordinance compelling plantations to make a contribution for the appointment of a European medical officer and a number of assistants for each district.

2. TRANSPORT AND COMMUNICATIONS

The growth of coffee plantations led to a remarkable development in transport and communications. The policy of road-construction was carried out with great zeal and a railway was established between Colombo and Kandy.

Sir George Anderson (1850-55), Sir Henry Ward (1855-1860), and Sir Hercules Robinson (1865-1872) took a keen interest in the plantations and continued to construct roads to help their development. Anderson resumed the work interrupted by the financial crisis of 1847. He wanted to build new roads to open up the country and to provide means for transporting the produce of the plantations from the interior to the sea-ports. As he could not carry out his objects fully for want of money, he decided to take up the roads one by one according to their importance, and to complete them in turn instead of spending money on several undertakings at the same time. According to this plan he completed the road from Gampola to Yatiyantota, a town already connected with Colombo, and afforded another outlet from the hills by way of Ginigathēna to Colombo. Ward improved this road from Kandy to Colombo by building bridges at Pērādeniya, Gampola, Nāvalapitiya and Kitulgala, besides constructing a road from Nāvalapitiya to Kotmalē,

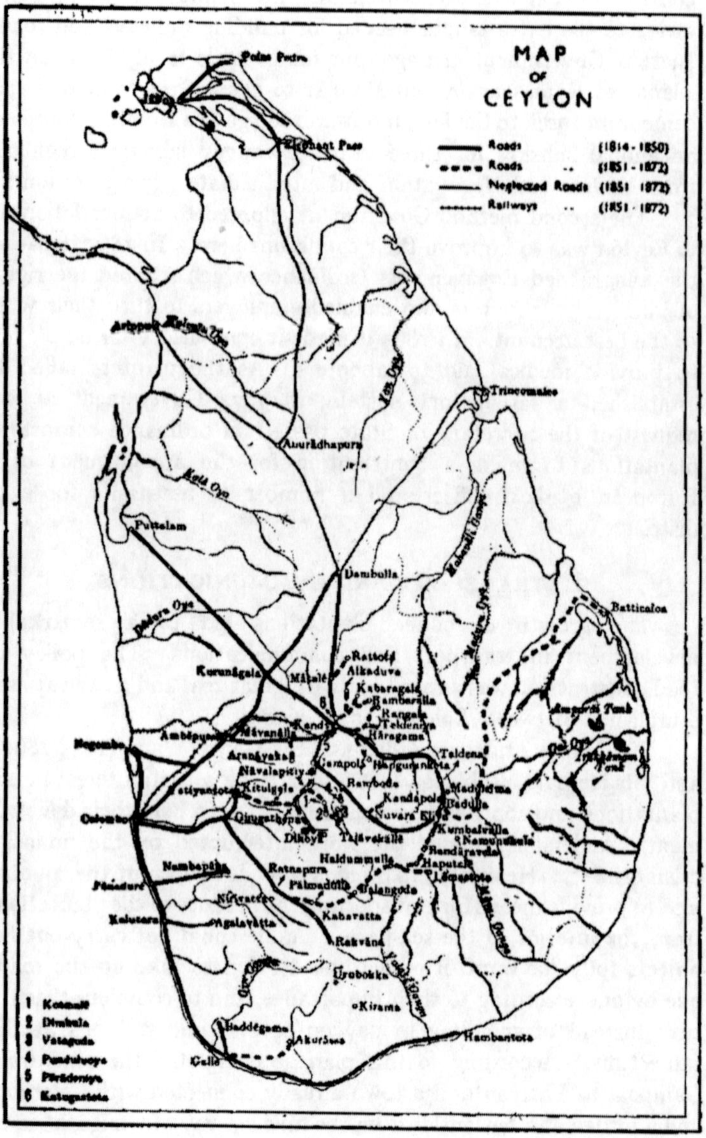
MAP OF CEYLON
Roads (1814-1850)
Roads (1851-1872)
Neglected Roads (1851 1872)
Railways (1851-1872)
Point Pedro
Elephant Pass
Trincomalee
Anurādhapura
Puttalam
Dambulla
Batticaloa
Kurunāgala
Mātalē
Kandy
Negombo
Colombo
Kalutara
Ratnapura
Badulla
Haputalē
Hambantota
Galle
Baddēgama
Akurēssa
Kirama
Rakvāna
Balangoda
Nuvara Eliya
Kitulgala
Pānadurē
Kala Oya
Deduru Oya
Mahaveli Ganga
1 Kotmalē
2 Dimbula
3 Vatagoda
4 Pundaluoya
5 Pērādeniya
6 Katugastota

and Robinson replaced the wooden bridge at Yatiyantota with an iron-girder lattice bridge. Robinson helped to develop further the area south of Kandy by building a road from Māvanälla in the direction of Aranāyaka to open up the district of Dolosbāgē. During this period Government concerned itself mainly with trunk roads, and the planters were expected to construct branch roads to their plantations. But the latter were dissatisfied with the arrangement, and Government agreed to construct branch roads if the plantations which were to benefit would pay half the cost of construction and maintenance. On this basis the Kandy-Ginigathēna Road was extended to Dikoya to provide the plantations there facilities for the transport of their produce. In Anderson's time a number of other new roads were opened in the cultivated parts of the Central Province. One of these was built by Jeronis de Soysa at his own expense.[1] The cost of the others was partly borne by the owners of plantations who benefited by them.

Ward helped to develop the region to the east of Kandy and Mātalē. He opened a road from Mātalē to Rattota, and another from Teldeniya to Rangala. This region contained thirty thousand acres of coffee in 1858 but its produce had to be transported to Kandy by inconvenient ferries across the Mahaväli Ganga. Ward further met the demands of the planters of the area by building a bridge at Teldeniya, connecting Kandy with Rangala and Mäda-mahanuvara. Another bridge he built at Katugastota served to link Mātalē and Kurunägala, centres of two other coffee districts, with Kandy, the hill capital and nodal point of the elaborate road system that was growing up in the coffee area. Robinson too helped to develop this area east of Kandy and Mātalē. He constructed through Katugastota one road which branched off in the directions of Bambaraälla and Kabaragala and another which went to Älkaduva, and extended the Kandy-Teldeniya Road as far as Galmal Oya.

1 Jeronis de Soysa was the father of the philanthropist C. H. de Soysa. He was a member of the Karava community the members of which, not being attached to land by occupation, were the first persons to take advantage of the new avenues of work offered by the plantations. At first he traded and carried out government contracts, and in 1835 bought the King's Garden at Hanguranketa, in which there was a considerable amount of coffee, as well as all the adjoining forest land. It is said that the first crop gave him much more than the £650 for which he had bought the King's Garden See Villiers: *Mercantile Lore*, p. 249.

Another region which began to develop during the period as a result of the construction of roads was the eastern part of Sabaragamuva and the province of Ūva. Road-building was arrested as the Secretary of State ordered the expenditure on public works to be curtailed in order to reduce the debt on the railway. So Sir Charles McCarthy (1860-1863) concentrated on maintaining existing roads rather than building new ones, but he could not resist the demands of the Haputalē planters. Ward had continued the Colombo-Ratnapura Road to Pälmadulla. McCarthy asked Skinner to extend it as far as Balangoda. Skinner carried out this work for half the estimated cost, and McCarthy allowed him to continue it another fifteen miles and bring it to the borders of Ūva.

Robinson extended the road to Älla, which was already connected with Badulla. Ward had improved the Colombo-Badulla Road via Kandy and Nuvara Eliya. But the Badulla District was being opened up quickly, and the planters wanted better access to Colombo. Robinson considered three proposals. He did not favour the restoration of the old Kandy-Badulla Road as it lay through barren and unhealthy country. He preferred the proposal to build a road through Valapanē via Uda Pussellāva as it would pass through a populous district and connect secluded villages, besides providing access to the coffee plantations of these districts; but this was rejected as it would have involved the construction of another road to the Madulsīma-Taldena area which was covered by the old road. He finally decided on the extension of the Colombo-Haputalē Road as it gave access to the plantations of the Namunukula District. He further improved the roads of this region by replacing the old wooden bridges at Nirivatta (near Ratnapura), Kahavatta (south of Pälmadulla) and Badulla with iron bridges, and that at Ratnapura with an iron-girder lattice bridge.

Robinson also built a road from Galle through Akurässa to open up Moravak Kōralē. This coffee area in the remote south, cut off from the rest of the coffee country of the central highlands, exported its produce for the most part through the port of Galle.

The coffee districts were not the only areas that received attention. Ward was anxious to improve the condition of the peasants, who had been neglected by his predecessors, and the general administration of the island. The main trunk roads built by Barnes and Horton had been neglected with the rise of the coffee industry. Of the road from Kandy which went from Dambulla northwards to Point Pedro and north-east to Trincomalee, only the part up to Mātalē which served the coffee plantations had been kept in repair. Ward improved the road as far as Dambulla, and continued the work undertaken by Anderson in the section between Jaffna and Elephant Pass, where European planters had invested capital in coconut plantations. Robinson extended the Colombo-Badulla Road via Haputalē to Batticaloa. This road opened up the Madulsīma coffee area, and for the first time Batticaloa, the chief town of the Eastern Province, as well as a region where a special effort was being made to develop paddy cultivation, was connected with Colombo. At this time the Northern and the Eastern Provinces were not easily accessible by land from the rest of the island, and steamers were the chief means of communication between Colombo and these provinces. The steamships were first run by Government, then by a company, and again by Government.

Thus there was great progress in road construction during this period. Roads helped to open up the district to the east of Kandy and Mātalē, and the area between Kandy and Hatton and the region of Eastern Sabaragamuva and Ūva. At the end of Ward's rule there were 3,000 miles of road in good repair, either wholly or partly macadamized. And at the end of this period most of the important towns of the island were connected by road with Colombo and Kandy.

It has been shown how the growth of plantations led to the construction of a large number of new roads. The need for a better and quicker means of transporting the produce of the plantations led to the establishment of the railway.

The earliest railways in the world, the English Stockton-Darlington Railway and the Liverpool-Manchester Railway had been established in 1825 and in 1830 respectively. Other projects had been started by railway companies from 1835, and Ceylon coffee merchants and planters wanted railways constructed here. In 1845 the building of a railway from Colombo to Kandy was seriously considered, and a company was formed in England for its construction. A survey of the line was made and the cost was estimated at £80,000. But the project was suspended owing to the coffee crash and the difficulty of obtaining a loan in England. With the revival of coffee in 1853, the year in which railways began to be constructed in India, merchants and planters again demanded the construction of a railway, and the Secretary of State resumed negotiations with the company formed in 1845 in order to enter into a contract with it.

In the meantime developments in Ceylon brought home to the planters the need for constructing a railway without delay. The export of coffee which was 278,473 cwt. in 1850 rose to 372,379 cwt. in 1853, and was expected to reach 500,000 cwt. in 1856. All this had to be conveyed to Colombo between the close of the picking season in January and the commencement of the south-west monsoon in May. Once the monsoon broke, roads which had no bridges over the streams they crossed became impassable, and the value of the coffee which could not be despatched was impaired.

Up to this time all coffee and plantation supplies were transported in bullock carts owned by Ceylonese. In 1854 about 30,000 to 36, 00 cart-loads were taken from Colombo to Kandy and back, and the pressure on the road was so great that a cart which normally returned in six to eight days took fourteen to eighteen days, and some carts even four to six weeks. The insufficiency of carts and the competition among the planters who were anxious to get their coffee conveyed to Colombo in time led to a rise in the cost of transport. The normal rate for a bullock cart which took half a load of rice to Kandy and returned with 10 cwt. of dried coffee was £3; but in 1854 before the monsoon the amount rose to £4. 10*s.*, while in some places accidents, cattle-sickness and the weather made it impossible to obtain carts at any price.

The planters found that their cost of production rose further as a result of the drought in India in 1854. They had to supply rice to their labourers at a fixed average price. A bushel of rice which normally cost 3*s.* 6*d.* to 4*s.* 6*d.* in Colombo rose this year to 7*s.* 6*d*; owing to difficulties of transport, it cost 10*s.* to 12*s.* in Kandy, 13*s.* to 14*s.* in Gampola. A labourer's wages for the conveyance of a bushel was 7*d.* a day, and a corresponding amount had to be added for rice supplied in the interior.

All these facts convinced the planters that no increase in the means of transport then in use could keep pace with the increase in production, and even if it were possible to procure the number of additional carts and bullocks that would have been required, no ordinary road could have afforded the necessary facilities. Moreover the planters feared that when railways were developed in Brazil, the price of coffee there would go down by 6*s*. to 8*s*. per cwt., and that Ceylon would not be able to compete with Brazil unless cheaper, regular communications were established between Colombo and the plantations.

In 1855 Ward considered the establishment of a railway an absolute and imperative necessity, and the Legislative Council unanimously agreed to the proposal that the Government of Ceylon should guarantee the 6 per cent. interest on a loan of £80,000. Acting in accordance with British ideas of government and policy at this time, the Secretary of State refused to permit the Ceylon Government to construct the line, and private companies refused to undertake the work without this security. In 1856 a provisional contract was signed and ratified by the Legislative Council, after much opposition from the unofficial members who thought it gave room to the Company to increase its rates. So another survey was made in 1857 and the total cost was estimated at £856,557

The construction of the railway was begun in 1858, but the work had to be interrupted after three years. After the work had been carried on for about a year, the Company completed a survey of its own, and announced that the railway would cost not £856,557 but £2,214,000. The result was that the Secretary of State, the Governor and the Company were bitterly attacked; and in spite of Ward's desire to continue the work, the Legislative Council in 1860 insisted on his annulling the contract. The Ceylon Government then undertook the construction of the railway; and unlike in India and in England, railways in Ceylon became a government concern. Work was resumed in 1863. In 1865 the railway reached Ambēpussa, and the line to Kandy was completed in 1867.

The construction of the roads and the railway helped the development not only of plantations and trade but also of the postal system. During this period an important reform was made in the matter of postage. Hitherto the rate charged for a letter depended not only on its weight but also on the distance it was carried. Whereas a letter half an ounce in weight sent to a place within twenty-five miles cost 2*d*. a letter sent to a spot more than 150 miles away cost 1*s*. In England Rowland Hill had shown that the cost of transporting letters depended on the collection, sorting and delivery and very little on the distance they were carried, and the rate of postage had been reduced in 1840 to the flat rate of a penny. Penny postage was adopted in Ceylon in 1858. The reduction of the rate not only increased the number of letters but also helped to develop business relationships and trade in general.

It was also in 1858 that the electric telegraph was introduced into Ceylon, and it linked not only the important towns of the island but also Ceylon with India and England. Cooke and Wheatstone had patented the electro-magnetic telegraph in 1837, and the first telegraph company in England had been formed in 1847. Eleven years later Colombo was connected by electric telegraph with Galle, and the pigeon service run by the *Colombo Observer* was discontinued. In the same year Colombo was connected also with Kandy and Mannār, and in 1865 with Trincomalee.

The construction of telegraph lines in India had begun in 1854, and the line to Mannār was extended in 1859 to India, connecting Colombo with Calcutta, Bombay and Madras. Soon after India was connected with England by an overland telegraph line, and in 1866 Robinson was able to communicate direct with the Secretary of State. This overland line proved unsatisfactory, and in 1870 a submarine cable was laid. Henceforth the Governor of Ceylon was able to communicate with the Secretary of State by cable without interruption.

The different parts of the island already connected by roads and the railway were linked more closely by the telegraph. It helped to improve the system of administration by giving the central government a greater control over the provinces. The submarine cable in turn increased the control of the Secretary of State, and brought Ceylon into close contact with movements in Europe.

3. IRRIGATION WORKS AND THE GANSABHĀVAS

The irrigation works which had been neglected for two decades received some attention from the time of Ward. In 1845 a Committee had been appointed to inquire into the system of irrigation. It had recommended the restoration of ancient tanks, and even suggested that some of the labour made available by the Road Ordinance should be applied to this purpose. But the Secretary of State, obsessed by British ideas of government at the time, refused to allow grants-in-aid to irrigation works unless they increased the productive powers of the island and were likely to yield a fair return on the capital invested, and objected to the labour made available by the Road Ordinance being used for such work.

Torrington and Anderson could not undertake the restoration of any irrigation works owing to the trade depression. Conditions had improved when Ward arrived. His attention was drawn both by government officials and the public to the wretched state of the irrigation works and he included their restoration in his scheme for developing the resources of the island by productive public works. In accordance with the instructions of the Secretary of State he restored the Irakkāmam and Amparai Tanks in the Batticaloa District, and the Kirama and the Ūrubokka works in the Giruva Pattuva of the Southern Province. All these proved in time successful. The mere sale of lands around Irakkāmam and Amparai Tanks met the expenditure on these two works. In 1864 the land under rice cultivation in the Batticaloa District was 77,000 acres.

Ward did not stop at the restoration of these larger tanks. He helped the repair of many smaller works in the Badulla and the Mātalē Districts and in some other parts of the Central Province. The most important of these were supervised by the trained officers of the Department of the Civil Engineer. The rest were repaired with the voluntary labour of the peasants under the control of Government, which contributed a part of the cost.

McCarthy curtailed all expenditure on public works and did little for irrigation, but Robinson showed no less interest than Ward in restoring irrigation works. In 1866 he appointed a Commission to report on them, and its recommendations for their development and the extension of paddy cultivation were accepted by the Legislative Council. In 1867 Government, in addition to the contribution of a share of the cost of smaller irrigation works, offered to give peasants advances to be repaid in ten annual instalments. Many villagers in the Southern and the Eastern Provinces, where paddy cultivation paid best, took advantage of this offer.

The restoration of irrigation works had important results. Though it did not bring about any such important economic change as the establishment of plantations and the construction of roads had done, it helped to develop certain regions especially in the Dry Zone, and provided the inhabitants of these areas with the means to enjoy a more satisfactory standard of living.

The restoration of irrigation works was a return to the ancient methods of government. At this time the process of modernizing the government of Ceylon went on. As before, according to developments in British ideas and practices, changes were made from time to time. But Government fully realized at this time that typically British methods of government could not always be applied to a country like Ceylon, where conditions differed profoundly from those in England. And steps were taken to revert to some of the old methods of government which were more suited to local conditions.

The most important change in this direction was the revival of the gansabhāvas. With the gradual restoration of the older irrigation system, Government gradually realized the important part played by them in the village economy. Bailey, who took a keen interest in irrigation, suggested re-establishing the old system of communal labour in the repair and upkeep of tanks and channels and in the cultivation of paddy. He proposed the revival of the old customs that governed irrigation and cultivation in the form of rules; and the grant of powers to the gansabhāvas, presided over by the Government Agent or his Assistant, to deal summarily with breaches of these rules and inflict fines up to £2. These proposals were also in accordance with the suggestion made in 1848 by the Secretary of State to follow Indian experience and entrust the repair and upkeep of village tanks to village communities. Ward accepted Bailey's recommendations and passed the Gansabhāva Ordinance of 1856. All Government Agents testified to the usefulness of the gansabhāvas thus established, and it was generally accepted that they specially suited an agricultural people who still followed a feudal or pre-feudal form of life, and whose needs could not be met by the new institutions.

In 1871 Robinson increased the powers of the gansabhāvas. Reference has been made to the large number of petty charges instituted in the courts as a result of the decline of the gansabhāvas. In 1869 there were charges against 168,426 persons. Of these 112,301 were dismissed without trial, while only a tenth of the accused were convicted. The villagers incurred heavy expenses in instituting these cases while their agriculture suffered by their absence from the village. To put an end to this state of affairs Robinson empowered the villagers to frame rules for the regulati n of purely village affairs, such as agriculture, fisheries, village sch ols and paths. The gansabhāvas, composed of five members chosen by lot from the chief landowners of the village with the chief of the district as president, were empowered to enforce these rules. He gave them also the authority to try all offences arising from acts against ancient customs as well as petty criminal and civil cases, and inflict fines up to £2. Their proceedings were to be summary and no lawyers were to appear, but an appeal was allowed to the Government Agent.

The new gansabhāvas proved a great success. They settled satisfactorily thousands of criminal and civil disputes and there were very few appeals against their decisions. Litigation too decreased. In many villages there was a change for the better Paths were cleared and wells were enclosed, school-houses were erected, burial places were assigned and kept freefrom jungle, cattle were registered and cattle-thieving was checked.

4. ADMINISTRATIVE REFORMS

During this period further steps were taken to make the administration more efficient, and to bring it into line with the demands made by the planters and the merchants. There was also some attempt to improve and to adapt the system of government to serve the interests of the peasants.

The reforms in the Civil Service made in 1845 were so far-reaching that few changes were found necessary. In 1857 candidates seeking admission to the Civil Service from England were required to sit for a competitive examination conducted by the Civil Service Commissioners. Hitherto they were selected mainly from the gentry, but this new method of recruitment gave a preponderance to recruits who had risen by reason of their learning from a somewhat different strata of society and lacked the traditions of paternal government with which the squirearchy had for long been associated. The standard of education of the new entrants was higher as only university graduates with a liberal education could take the subjects prescribed for the examination. A corresponding change was made in the method of recruitment in Ceylon. Those who were hitherto appointed by nomination were required in 1863 to pass a non-competitive examination, and from 1870 the Civil Service Examination was held simultaneously in England and in Ceylon to enable Ceylonese to sit for the same examination as the British candidates. In 1867 steps were also taken to see that the candidates who came from England acquired a sufficient knowledge of Sinhalese and Tamil.

The modification in the system of Provincia' Administration after 1833 was continued. Puttalam, the capital of the North-Western Province, was important only on account of its salt industry. In 1856 Kurunāgala, which was more central and had become more important owing to the cultivation of coffee in the surrounding area, was made the capital of the Province; and Puttalam was reduced to an Assistant Agency. Trincomalee had been made the capital of the Eastern Province for its valuable harbour whose importance had now waned. In 1870 Batticaloa, which was in an area more thickly populated and was being connected by road with Colombo, was made the capital of the Province and Trincomalee became an Assistant Agency.

The administration of the districts improved further as Government's attitude towards headmen gradually changed during this period. After the disturbances of 1848 Government realized that it could not rule the country efficiently unless it trusted them. Since the chiefs themselves no longer opposed British rule, it sought their co-operation, and restored to them some of the powers of which they had been deprived. In 1874 it increased the power of the chief headmen by making them presidents of the gansabhāvas of their district with power to overrule the other members. They thus became responsible for all minor matters in their districts and regained part of the power they exercised in ancient times, and the Government Agents lost to a great extent what direct touch they used to have with the people.

In 1860 further steps were taken to separate the judicial and revenue duties in all places of importance, for example planting centres like Mātalē, Ratnapura and Kurunāgala. So before long judicial and revenue duties were combined only in backward towns like Anurādhapura, Mannār, Mullaitīvu, Trincomalee, Puttalam, Hambantota and Nuvara Eliya, in which places British interests played no important part.

There were a few judicial reforms in the interests of the poorer classes. To relieve the congestion of work in the District Courts and to grant speedy justice, Police Courts had been established in 1844 to deal with petty crimes, and Courts of Requests in 1848 to deal with petty civil disputes. In 1852 the jurisdiction of the Court of Requests was extended to give litigants a cheap and simple, yet efficient, means of obtaining justice in such matters as land suits. Land disputes often led to acts of violence, mainly on account of the lack of a cheap and speedy method of settlement. In the time of Sir Henry Ward (1855-1860) Itinerating Courts were established and judicial divisions were redistributed for the convenience of suitors who had sometimes to travel far to attend court.

The process of bringing the laws of Ceylon in line with those of England was carried further during this period. The system of Roman-Dutch Law did not satisfy the requirements of the commercial class, and in 1852 on the recommendation of the Chamber of Commerce the laws of England began to be applied to all matters connected with shipping and other maritime affairs, and questions regarding bills of exchange, promissory notes and cheques. Some time later the laws of Ceylon were further assimilated with those of England in matters relating to the law of partnership, joint-stock companies corporations, banks and banking, principals and agents, carriers by land, and life and fire insurance. In 1852 it was also decided to assimilate the laws of the Kandyan Provinces with those of the Maritime Provinces and to make them as uniform as possible. Roman-Dutch Law was introduced into the Kandyan Provinces in all suits where the old Kandyan or Sinhalese law afforded no ruling.

5. LEGISLATIVE AND LOCAL COUNCILS

The agitation for the reform of the Legislative Council was continued during this period mainly owing to the dissatisfaction, especially on the part of merchants and planters, with Government over questions of transport. During the years 1848 to 1855 they made a demand for an unofficial majority in order to control Government. Owing to the decline of the coffee industry after the crisis of 1847, Government was compelled to reduce its expenditure; and the merchants and planters were dissatisfied with the appropriations granted for the maintenance and construction of roads. When the revival of the coffee industry enabled Government to increase its expenditure once more, the agitation died down.

A demand for the control of the Council was made again in 1859 by the British colonists and the Burghers mainly owing to the collapse of the government plans for building the railway from Colombo to Kandy.

These requests for the reform of the Legislative Council were refused for the same reasons as before. It was said that if representative or responsible government were introduced in Ceylon, the executive would be controlled by some seven or eight thousand Europeans and the Burghers; and the needs of the two million Sinhalese, Tamils, and Muslims, who could not be adequately represented would be neglected. However the agitation had one result. Unofficial members were given the right to introduce bills, hitherto considered an exclusive right of Government.

The demand for an unofficial majority in the Legislative Council was revived again in 1865 when the unofficials failed to have their way over the question of the military contribution. Since 1838 Ceylon had paid annually £24,000 as a contribution to the British Exchequer on account of the troops stationed in Ceylon in addition to other sums, amounting to more than double this amount, spent by the Government of Ceylon on military buildings and various other allowances. The Imperial Government had demanded this payment under the impression that for several years there had been a large surplus of revenue over expenditure in Ceylon. On the contrary in 1838 Government badly needed money to provide roads to the recently opened estates, and the Governor and the Legislative Council had tried every possible method to obtain an exemption from the payment but had failed. Later the amount had been increased, and in 1864 the total military contribution of Ceylon was half the annual military expenditure of £200,000. The finances of the island had been improving again after the revival of the coffee industry. But Government had been cutting down expenditure in order to finance the railway from Colombo to Kandy, and as a result of this economy the revenue had been exceeding expenditure by an increasing amount each year, till in 1864 the excess for the year was as much as £100,000. The Colonists were bitter about the economy which had created this result. The Imperial Government, on the other hand, looked at things in a very different light and in 1861 Parliament had resolved that all colonies should as far as possible bear the entire cost of the garrisons maintained in them for purposes of their own defence. In accordance with this Ceylon in 1864 was called upon to pay an annual contribution of £135,000 rising by £10,000 per year until the amount reached the total military expenditure. At the same time the Secretary of State promised to grant the Legislative Council control over the budget when it passed an ordinance providing the military expenditure, fixed upon by a committee of inquiry consisting of official and unofficial members of the Council.

The unofficial members of the Legislative Council opposed the increase on military expenditure. They pointed out that a large part of the garrison was maintained for imperial purposes and not for the protection of Ceylon. They expressed their willingness to pay a reasonable sum determined by the Legislative Council and not by the Secretary of State, since the right to control the budget had been accepted in 1848. When Government with the Official majority provided the contribution required, the unofficials resigned in a body and refused to co-operate with Government.[1]

Legally the unofficials were in the wrong. It has already been pointed out that in 1839 the Legislative Council was permitted to criticize the annual contingent expenditure without interfering with the fixed civil and military expenditure. In 1848 the Secretary of State had accepted the principle that the budget should be controlled by the Legislative Council and had informed the Governor that this control would be handed over when an ordinance was passed making a permanent charge upon the funds of the Colony for the 'fixed' portion of the civil and military expenditure. In 1858 a Fixed Establishments Ordinance had been passed for the annual payment of the civil expenditure, but nothing had been done with regard to the military expenditure. The action of the unofficials has to be traced to deeper causes. Since 1861 the Europeans had been dissatisfied with Government's interest in roads. They held the view that the surpluses should be spent on roads or that the taxes ought to be reduced. The Burghers were disappointed with the share of higher appointments in the Government service granted to them.

In 1865 the Europeans and the Burghers formed the Ceylon League in order to secure an unofficial majority in the Legislative

1 The non-co-operators were C. A. Lorenz, George Wall, W. Thompson, James Capper, James de Alwis and J. H. Eaton.

Council. The League carried on the agitation in Ceylon and in England, but the Secretary of State refused to grant its demands. With the return of prosperity, road construction was resumed and the agitation died down. In 1867 the recommendations of the Military Commission appointed to determine Ceylon's contribution towards its defence were accepted, and an ordinance was passed fixing it at £160,000. The Secretary of State then gave the Legislative Council the control of the budget.

Councils to deal with local affairs were established during this period. Like the Legislative Council, it was not due to a demand by the inhabitants of Ceylon that local councils were established. As the British people had begun to realize that epidemics in towns were due mainly to dirt and overcrowding and that sanitation was a public responsibility, Parliament has passed in 1848 a Public Health Act establishing a General Board of Health. In 1853 there was an outbreak of small-pox in Ceylon, and the Ceylon Government established Local Boards of Health to take sanitary precautions in towns.

There were few towns in Ceylon before the British occupation and their population was comparatively small. But the growth of plantations and the development of trade and transport led to the growth of Colombo, Kandy and Galle, and the rise of a number of small towns in planting centres where traders and craftsmen congregated. Colombo rose in importance as it continued to be the seat of government and the chief port for the export of Ceylon produce. Kandy, lying in the midst of the plantations, became their chief distributing centre since the completion of the Colombo-Kandy Road. Galle continued to be important as the port of call for steamers on their way to or from the Far East and Australia.

In 1865 another ordinance was passed to establish municipal councils in the chief towns of the island. Under the Portuguese Colombo had been governed by a chamber of elected members which had exercised some of the rights and privileges of a Portuguese *cidade*. This form of government had disappeared with the Dutch conquest. At first the British, following the practice in their own country, did indeed act upon the principle that expenditure for certain purely local purposes like the repairs and lighting of streets within a town must be met from funds assessed upon the householders of the town and not from the general funds of the Colony. The same principle was to apply to some extent even with regard to the Police force stationed in Colombo and the other towns. But in the total absence of municipal institutions the assessment taxes were collected and the local expenditure was managed by the central government. Robinson, in whose time this ordinance was passed, had in view mainly the sanitary improvement of towns and the check of epidemic diseases. His object was to give the chief citizens of the towns the power and the funds, not only to keep the streets in repair and provide them with lights, but also to supply them with pure water, with markets where the sale of foodstuffs could be supervised and controlled, and with slaughter-houses to prevent cattle and goats being killed in the premises of butchers' shops situated in the heart of the town. As a result of this ordinance, municipal councils were established in Colombo and in Kandy in 1866 and in Galle in 1867, and in a few years conditions in the towns improved.

Another of Robinson's objects in passing this ordinance of 1865 was to afford the citizens of the towns a training in exercising a measure of political power. He was probably influenced by the reform agitation. The Liberals in England at this time certainly did believe in training people in the art of government. So the Colombo Council was given ten elected and nine nominated members, and the Kandy and Galle Councils five elected and four nominated members each. In the Colombo Council a Civil Servant was appointed as full-time chairman, while the Government Agents of the Central and Southern Provinces presided over the Kandy and Galle Councils as a part of their duties.

6. EDUCATION

In India at the beginning of this period the need for extending Western learning to all classes of the population was emphasized, and departments of education were established in the provinces, and universities in the cities of Calcutta, Bombay and Madras. But in Ceylon the need for ensuring that education kept pace with modern knowledge to enable the people to benefit from the changes made by Government was not recognized as strongly as before. Four reasons probably accounted for this. The existing English schools supplied the number of persons needed for the subordinate services of Government. Many people considered English to be unsuitable as a medium of instruction for Sinhalese and Tamil children. A foreign government could not be expected to keep up its interest in education when even in Britain the Government did not make itself responsible for the education of its people till the year 1870. Moreover the spread of English education led to inconvenient demands for the reform of the Legislative Council, and these were viewed with disfavour by the Government of Ceylon.

Reference has been made to retrenchment in education during the depression of 1847-1850. Enough was not done to improve matters even when conditions changed; and the schools and pupils under Government were still less in number than those in charge of the Missions. In 1868 Government had only eighteen English schools with 1,908 pupils, and forty-one Anglo-vernacular schools with 1,949 pupils. However there were sixty-three Government vernacular schools with 3,624 pupils, but the standard of these schools had deteriorated with the closing of the Normal School in 1857. The reports of Sendall, Inspector of Schools, show that the standard of English education was no better.

The School Commission had gradually lost its authority and become an advisory body to the Colonial Secretary. Already unpopular owing to the way it managed the education of the island, it courted further disfavour by its attitude towards religious instruction in schools. A notable despatch of 1854 had recommended grants to Christian schools in India, and in 1857 the Anglican Bishop of Colombo had asked for similar grants to Christian schools in Ceylon. The Legislative Council approved of his request provided religious instruction was made optional. But the Missions objected to any restrictions, and the Commission supported them against the Council.

General dissatisfaction with the state of education in the island led to the appointment of a Committee in 1865. This Committee made a comprehensive survey of the system of education in Ceylon and issued its report in 1867. A number of changes were made on its recommendations. In 1870 the School Commission was abolished and replaced by a Department of Public Instruction responsible to the Governor. Government undertook the responsibility for vernacular education and set about its extension immediately. The number of Government schools, which in 1870 was 156 with 8,726 pupils, rose in 1872 to 200 with 10,852 pupils. Grants-in-aid were paid to all schools which gave a sound secular education, and in order to satisfy the Christian missionary bodies no restrictions were laid on religious instruction. The Missions began to expand their educational work at once. Their schools, which in 1870 numbered

229 with 8,201 pupils, rose in 1872 to 402 schools (including sixty-four Roman Catholic schools) with 25,443 pupils. A Normal School was stablished by Government for the training of teachers for English, Anglo-vernacular and vernacular schools. Of the Colombo Academy the upper section which prepared students for the Calcutta University examinations was abolished as its numbers did not justify its continuance. Instead, from the year 1870, after the Suez Canal was opened, promising students were awarded scholarships to continue their studies at a British university

Thus education was removed from the control of the Missions and placed under the direct control of Government. Colebrooke's recommendation that Government should be responsible for English education was reversed. The extension of the grant-in-aid system to all efficient non-Government schools accelerated the spread of education and prepared the way for Buddhists and Hindus to establish their own schools. The standard of teaching in schools was raised by establishing an institution for the training of teachers. And for higher education Ceylon began to look to England instead of to India.

7. THE CHRISTIAN MISSIONS, BUDDHISM AND HINDUISM

The Christian Missions made great headway during this period In the sixties the Baptist, the Wesleyan, the American, and the Church Missionary Societies celebrated the jubilees of their work in Ceylon, and carried on their evangelistic work more zealously than ever before. Those who realized the value of education at this time welcomed Christian schools, while the Missions found schools a good means for spreading Christianity. They also influenced people by direct preaching as well as through newspapers, magazines, books and tracts.

These activities produced certain reactions. An impetus was given to the revival of Buddhism and Hinduism which were awakening from their long slumber. Buddhism reached its lowest ebb during Portuguese times. Its revival, led by Välivita Saranankara (1698-1778) in the Kandyan Kingdom, had its effects at first only within that area. But those in pupilary succession to Saranankara gradually went to the Maritime Provinces and revived Buddhist studies in vihārēs chiefly in the Southern Province, where Dutch

Christian influence was weakest. In 1839 the Paramadhammacētiya Pirivena was established at Ratmalāna by Valānē Siddhartha of Pānadurē, and there passed out of this educational institution a number of scholars such as Hikkaduvē Srī Sumangala (1826-1911), Ratmālanē Dharmāloka (1827-1887) and his pupil Srī Dharmārāma (1853-1918), and Pandit Batuvantudāvē Devarakshita (1819-1892).

The bhikshus and the laymen who studied at Buddhist centres of learning and others who studied at Government and Mission schools carried on various controversies in journals and newspapers, like the *Lakmini Pahana* (1862), which came into being during this period. A controversy which started in the early fifties dealt with the impiety of monks and the propriety of giving them alms. Some years later in 1865 was established the Rāmanya Nikāya, the bhikshus of which claimed to follow the pure Buddhism of the Pāli Canon.

There were also controversies between Buddhists and Christians. At first Buddhists raised no serious opposition to Christian propaganda. Being a monastic religion Buddhism, unlike the Christian church, had no organization which linked the bhikshus and the laity. In earlier times the Sangha had not opposed the development of Hindu practices among the laity, and had the Christian missionaries merely preached Christianity, they might have been allowed to carry on their work without any serious opposition. But the Christian policy of forming those who came under their influence into a separate community which took no part in Buddhist rites and ceremonies made the Sangha realize that their ancestral religion was in danger. Individual bhikshus had earlier discussed their respective faiths with missionaries privately. They now began to enter into public discussions, and derived much encouragement by the controversies held at Baddēgama, at Varāgoda (Kālaniya) in 1865, at Udanvita (near Rambukkana) in 1866, and at Gampola in 1871.

The Buddhist bhikshus did not stop at public controversy They began to follow the methods of the missionaries themselves to counteract their evangelistic work. Assisted by Buddhist laymen who had acquired wealth by taking part in the new enterprises provided by British rule, they began to establish printing presses, publish tracts, and form societies for Buddhist propaganda. Before the end of this period a Buddhist vernacular school was established at Dodandūva, on lines similar to those of Mission schools.

The activities of the Christian missionaries in the North gave an impetus both to Tamil studies and to the revival of Hinduism. The Vaddukkodai Seminary not only maintained a high standard of education in English but also taught Tamil classics and Hindu philosophy. Two of its students, Thamotherampillai and Carroll Visvanāthapillai, who were successful at the first B.A. examination of the University of Madras in 1857, were Tamil scholars of no mean repute. Thamotherampillai, who edited ancient Tamil works, and another Seminary student, Velupillai, were in turn the head of Tamil studies in the Madras Presidency College. Kanakasabhaipillai, the author of *Tamils Eighteen Hundred Years Ago*, was a son of Carroll Visvanāthapillai.

But the revival of Hinduism which had suffered for three centuries under foreign rule, owed much to a pupil of the Methodist Central School (now Central College), Jaffna. After his school career Ārumuka Nāvalar became a teacher of the school. There he learnt the methods, organization and propaganda of the missionaries. In fact he was employed by them as a translator and in writing Christian tracts. Realizing later that he was being used to christianize Hindus, he gave up his work under the missionaries to spread Saivism and oppose the propagation of Christianity. He too carried on controversies with Christians and helped to develop modern Tamil prose, just as Sinhalese controversialists helped to develop modern Sinhalese prose. In 1872 he opened a rival English school at Vannarponnai in Jaffna in order to provide education to Hindu children in a Hindu school. In this way the first reactions against Western civilization showed themselves.

Reference has been made to the attempts made by Government to disentangle itself from Buddhism and the difficulties that arose in finding a suitable authority to take its place. When the proposals of Campbell were rejected, Government had to make some other arrangement, and in 1851 the Secretary of State allowed Anderson to make appointments till such arrangements were made.

In 1853 the Buddhists were provided with an organization to control their affairs. The bhikshus of each vihārē were allowed to appoint their own nāyaka thēra (chief monk). The Ratēmahatmayas and the Kōrālas of the districts in which the dēvālēs were situated were given the power to appoint their Basnāyaka Nilamēs. The selection of the Diyavadana Nilamē was left to the Basnāyaka Nilamēs and the Ratēmahatmayas of certain districts. Once the appointments were made, Government issued an instrument recognizing the titles of the parties.

This arrangement proved altogether unsatisfactory. Once the incumbents and Nilamēs were elected, they virtually became owners of property, and the other Buddhists who had no pecuniary interests in vihāra or dēvāla lands could not question their actions before a court of law. Moreover, by the rules of their Order Buddhist bhikshus were not permitted to meddle in worldly affairs.

It has been pointed out that Government at this time did not consider either the Sinhalese or the Tamils fit to take a share in governing the country. The Kandyans were the most backward at this time and were least fit to manage modern modes of government. The result was that the wrong type of man was often chosen, vihārēs and dēvālēs were neglected, and their property was frittered away by the irresponsible persons who had charge of them.

'In handing over Buddhism to its professors', said Gladstone, 'our duty is to give it an honest working constitution' This duty was omitted.

CHAPTER VIII

THE DEVELOPMENT OF THE COUNTRY AND THE IMPROVEMENT OF THE PEOPLE (1873-1890)

1. PLANTATIONS AND LABOUR

IT has been noticed that the coffee industry reached its peak of prosperity in 1870. The price of coffee rose by 50 per cent. during the next few years. This in turn led to the cultivation of the largest remaining forest reserve in the highlands known as the Wilderness of the Peak, extending from Nuvara Eliya through a succession of upland valleys in Dimbula, Dikoya, and Maskeliya to the Adam's Peak range. Between 1869 and 1879 over 400,000 acres of crown land were sold, and the area covered by European plantations rose in 1878 to 275,000 acres.

But before 1890 coffee ceased to be an important industry in the island. In 1869 the trees had begun to be attacked by a minute fungus called *Hemileia Vastatrix*. No one at first paid any serious attention to it as it did little harm to the crops. Even when the crops began to decrease the loss was not sufficiently noticed owing to the high price and the increased production. The result was that by 1882 the disease gradually spread over the whole area diminishing production till the exports of coffee quickly fell. In 1881 the exports had decreased to 436,881 cwt., which was less than that for 1854. In 1889 they sank further to 76,416 cwt. and the area under cultivation dwindled to about 50,000 acres

The decline of the coffee industry was due to other causes too. The increase in the price of coffee had to led to its extensive cultivation in Brazil, and the subsequent increase in the quantity imported into Europe led to a heavy fall in the price paid for Ceylon coffee. The plantations that were adversely affected by this fall in price and by the coffee pest needed further credit, but could not obtain it owing to the trade depression that prevailed in Europe during the years 1876-80. The good seasons which helped cultivation in the early seventies were followed by bad seasons in the later seventies. These factors led to the ruin of many plantations. Many of them were offered for sale but found no buyers. Ultimately out of the 1,700 European planters who lost their investments or posts or both, about 400 left Ceylon.

Another disaster that followed the collapse of the industry was the failure of the Oriental Bank Corporation in 1884. The bank from its very inception had financed the plantations, and could not now face their sudden ruin. At this time Government did not issue paper money, and currency notes were issued by banks. So the failure of the Bank would have affected a very large number of people who had no interest in the coffee industry. Gordon saved the situation by guaranteeing the Bank's notes, a step which cost the Government over Rs. 3,000. But the Imperial Government did not approve his action. Fearing that future Governors might follow this precedent under similar circumstances, reversing the policy hitherto followed, it permitted the Ceylon Government to issue notes. Thereupon in the same year the Ceylon Government passed the Ceylon Paper Currency Ordinance which led to the first issue of Government notes.

The failure of coffee affected the whole island. Planting enterprises had effected radical changes in the country. They had given employment to thousands and developed trade within and with other countries. The revenue of Ceylon which amounted to £372,000 in 1837 had risen in 1877 to Rs. 17,026,191. Export and import trade had risen from about £500,000 to about £10,000,000. This prosperity, which was mainly due to the plantations, had enabled the construction of roads and railways and helped the progress of the country as a whole. But the revenue went down with the decline of the coffee industry till in 1882 it sank to Rs. 12,161,570, and Government was compelled to curtail expenditure on all items that contributed to the advance of the country.

However this state of affairs did not last long. The decline of coffee led to the cultivation of other products. In 1861 the Royal Botanic Gardens had established a cinchona plantation at Hakgala and drawn the attention of the planters to it in 1867. In 1872 Ceylon cinchona which covered 500 acres had fetched the highest price in London. Yet in 1877 there were only 6,000 acres under cultivation owing to the large profits fetched by coffee. But with the failure of coffee in 1879 many rushed to cultivate cinchona, and the area covered by it soon rose to 60,000 acres. But the enormous exports of cinchona bark from Ceylon and Java, which too was affected by the coffee pest, exceeded the demand and the price began to fall. The result was that from 1884 the planters began to turn to other products, and cinchona gradually became a minor industry.

The Royal Botanic Gardens had experimented with tea even earlier. In 1845 it had established a small plantation, and in 1867 it had commissioned a planter to report on the tea industry in India. But planters had not taken to tea owing to the high profits in coffee, and in 1873 there were only 250 acres under cultivation. With the decline of coffee the area under tea rose in 1883 to 35,000 acres, and owing to the fall in the price of cinchona the acreage doubled in 1884. In 1887 it rose to 150,000 and in 1890 to 220,000, and the exports in 1889 rose to 34,345,852 lb. or one-third of the total exports.

Attempts were made to cultivate cocoa in Mātalē, Kurunāgala, and Ūva districts but they did not succeed as well as the attempts to grow tea The cultivation of the sugar-cane plant was tried at Baddēgama, but like all previous efforts met with no lasting success.

Labour did not cause any serious problems during this period. The scheme for medical aid laid down in 1872 however proved a failure. On the recommendations of a commission appointed by Government in 1878, the plantations were in 1883 grouped into districts and were provided by Government with hospitals and dispensaries manned by medical officers and assistants, many of whom had been trained at the Medical College established in 1870 The plantations contributed to the expenditure incurred by Government through a payment on behalf of every labourer that received attention at the government institutions, as well as by the payment of a tax of ten cents per cwt. on coffee, tea and cocoa exported and twenty cents per cwt. on cinchona.

2. TRANSPORT AND COMMUNICATIONS

The development of roads, railways, and telegraphs was continued during this period. All the Governors took an interest in plantations and aided the construction of roads and railways in plantation areas. Influenced probably by the growing interest in the British Isles in rural welfare, they also developed other areas for the benefit of the peasants.

Reference has already been made to the construction of a road from Ginigathena to Dickoya with the aid of a Government grant. Sir William Gregory (1872-1877) helped to develop the region further by extending this road to Maskeliya in order to open up the area near Adam's Peak. He also assisted with a similar grant the construction of a road from Kandapola to St. Margaret's to connect Uda Pussellāva with Nuvara Eliya by another grant-in-aid road giving the planters and villagers of this area an outlet for their produce. James Longden (1877-1883) curtailed public works owing to the fall in revenue as a result of the coffee disease, but built a few more roads in this area. As the railway was expected to reach Nānuoya shortly, in 1878 he began the approach roads. He extended the Dimbula Road to Nānuoya, and built another connecting Nuvara Eliya and Nānuoya to enable the produce of Dimbula and Uda Pussellāva to be despatched by train. The finances of the country had begun to improve when Sir Arthur Gordon (1883-1890) arrived, and he continued the development of this area. He connected Bōgavantalāva with Hatton by building a branch road from Norwood on the Hatton-Maskeliya road, and by another connected Punduluoya with Vatagoda. In 1890 the Kandy-Telden ya road, which had been extended to Galmal Oya by Robinson, was continued up to the Nugatänna gap, and from there northwards as far as Deanstone.

The Ratnapura district was further opened up during this period. Gregory extended the road from Mādampē to Rakvāna as far as Bulutota in order to give access to Kukulu Kōralē and to help the development of coffee in this area. To develop the area further Gordon built a branch road from the Ratnapura-Pälmadulla road in the direction of Kalavāna. In the Kalutara district Matugama on the Kalutara-Agalavatta road was connected with Nāboda. The Kalu Ganga was sufficiently deep at all seasons for the use of a steamer up to Nambapāna, and the Panadure-Nambapāna road was extended to Ratnapura to help the produce of Sabaragamuva to be carried by water from Nambapāna to Kalutara and thence by rail to Colombo. The road built by Robinson from Galle via Akurässa was extended by Gordon in order to open up the coffee area of Moravak Kōralē.

The development of plantations was not the only object in constructing roads. Gregory built a road in Pasdun Kōralē from Matugama to Välipānna to help owners of plumbago-mines to transport their ore. He also built a number of other roads to open up the backward parts of the island and to make them accessible to government officials and traders. The chief among these were the trunk roads from Dambulla to Jaffna and to Trincomalee respectively. At the beginning of Gregory's rule they had deteriorated into little

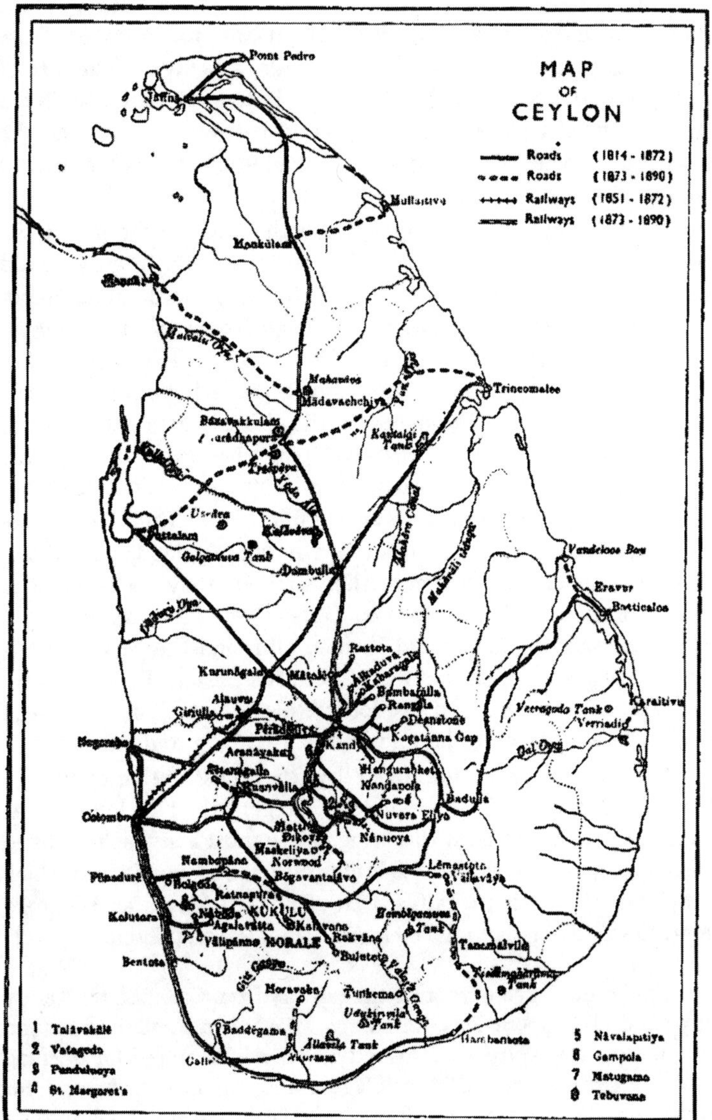
MAP
OF
CEYLON
Roads (1814 - 1872)
Roads (1873 - 1890)
Railways (1851 - 1872)
Railways (1873 - 1890)
Point Pedro
Mullaitivu
Trincomalee
Vandeloos Bay
Eravur
Batticaloa
Karaitivu
Mädavachchiya
Dambulla
Puttalam
Kurunägala
Rattota
Bambarälla
Deanstone
Kogatänna Gap
Badulla
Nuvara Eliya
Nänuoya
Hatton
Dikoya
Maskeliya
Norwood
Bogavantalävo
Negombo
Colombo
Nambapäna
Pänadurē
Ratnapura
Kalutara
Välipänne
Bentota
Moravaka
Baddēgama
Galle
Hambantota
Tanamalvila
1 Talāvakälë
2 Vatagoda
3 Pundaluoya
4 St. Margaret's
5 Nävalapitiya
6 Gampola
7 Matugama
8 Tebuvana

more than jungle paths with neither culverts nor bridges, impassable in rainy weather. From the trunk road to Jaffna Gregory built branch roads to Mullaitīvu from Mānkulam, to Puttalam from Anurādhapura, and to Mannār from Mādavachchiya. The last of these provided a route for labourers from India. Gordon completed this road in 1884 by building a causeway between Mannār and the mainland, and in 1886 he built the road from Anurādhapura to Trincomalee.

Gregory took steps to open up further the southern and the eastern part of the island. Robinson had built a grant-in-aid road as far as Lēmastota branching off from the Haldumulla-Haputalē road. Gregory extended this through Koslanda to Vällavāya, Tanamalvila and Hambantota. This road helped the coffee plantations of the Koslanda area and facilitated the traffic in salt between the Southern Province and the central parts of the island. It rendered also a service in developing the fever-stricken area which it traversed. Gregory also completed the Colombo-Batticaloa road, and from Eravur he built a branch road to Vandeloos Bay (Kalkudah). Vessels could not safely land and unload goods at Batticaloa throughout the year, but they could do so at Vandeloos Bay. Thus Batticaloa District was given an outlet by road to a seaport which could be used all round the year. In the time of Gordon another road was built in the Eastern Province from Karatīvu to Veeriadi. To Gordon are also due the roads between Ruanvälla and Attanagalla and between Giriulla and Alavva.

Many roads were improved by the construction of bridges during this period. Of those built by Gregory the best known is at Kalutara. Longden built the bridge at Grand Pass which replaced the old bridge of boats, and the bridge over the Elephant Pass which completed the road to Jaffna. In 1890 the bridges at Digarolla (Moratuwa), Bolgoda and Tebuvana were also completed.

The results of constructing the railway from Colombo to Kandy surpassed all expectations, and steps were taken in 1871 to extend the line to Nāvalapitiya. This extension was favoured for opening up the region between Pidurutalāgala and Adam's Peak, and for increasing the productiveness of the existing estates by affording them a cheaper means of transport for their manure. The line was opened to Gampola in 1873 and was extended to Nāvalapitiya in

1874. Gregory wanted to continue the line further, but the extension was begun only in 1880. It reached Hatton in 1884 and Nānu-oya in 1885.

Gregory planned the construction of two other lines. The one to Mātalē was begun in 1878 and opened to traffic in 1880 to serve the extensive plantations of this area. The Coast Line was opened up to Pānadurē in 1877 and extended in 1879 to Kalutara and in 1890 to Bentota. It was built to improve the rich and prosperous districts along which it passed, but it was used at first more for the conveyance of passengers rather than of goods.

The other means of transport used during the period were the canal between Puttalam and Colombo, the Kälani and the Kalu-Ganga with the Dutch canal that connected them, and the canal from Bolgoda Lake to the sea near Pānadurē constructed in 1879.

Telegraphic communication too was extended during this period. In 1874 Colombo was connected with Polgahavela, Kuru-nāgala and Anurādhapura, and in 1876 with Badulla and Batticaloa. Lines were also constructed to Negombo in 1887, to Ratnapura in 1888, to Mātara in 1889, and from Negombo to Puttalam in 1890. Thus almost all the important towns of the island were connected by telegraph, and these lines helped to improve the administration and to expand trade.

3 THE CONSTRUCTION OF THE COLOMBO HARBOUR

Perhaps the greatest event of this period was the construction of the Colombo harbour. Reference has been made to the effects of the establishment of plantations on the development of trade. Roads were built to transport the produce of the plantations to Colombo. The construction of the railway from Colombo to the highlands provided a cheaper and quicker means of transport. The next requirement was a satisfactory harbour in Colombo for the shipment of Ceylon produce. Gregory satisfied this need by building a breakwater. The work, begun in 1873, was completed in 1882 in the time of Longden.

Colombo had been the principal port of the island for trade from the days when the export of cinnamon had become considerable, and its importance had increased with the development of the plantations after the British occupation. But it was only a roadstead. Its bay had not sufficient depth to allow large vessels to lie alongside of the quay. A bar of sand, on some parts of which the water was not ten feet deep, extended from the projecting rock across the bay. The channel by which this bar was crossed was liable to shift and was not easily perceivable. So ships commonly anchored about a mile beyond it and ventured to enter the bay only in fine weather, and that too only in the safe season during the north-east monsoon. During the south-west monsoon from April to September communication between the shore and the ships was frequently interrupted, and was uncertain even during the best weather.

In these circumstances Galle had continued to be the most frequented harbour of the island. In Dutch times and in the early days of British rule the cinnamon of the Galle and Mātara districts was exported from Galle, and with the decline of the cinnamon trade Galle harbour ceased to have local trade of any consequence. But with the revival of the Mediterranean route it grew again in importance. It became an essential link in the chain of steam communication between England and Bombay on the one side and Calcutta, the Straits Settlements, China, Japan, Australia and New Zealand on the other.

The construction of the Suez Canal, which was opened to traffic on November 17, 1869, made Galle harbour still more important. Thenceforth ships came from London to Galle in about three weeks. The cost of transport immediately fell, and there followed a complete revolution in the carrying trade of the Eastern seas. In 1868 only 34 steamers entered Galle harbour. The number rose to 58 in 1869, 82 in 1870 and 110 in 1871. It was anticipated that the number would rise still further, and that steamers would before long replace the sailing vessels which plied round the Cape.

This increase in the number of steamers raised a new problem. In 1869 the exposed anchorage of the Galle harbour had proved inadequate to accommodate the ships that came there. If this inadequacy led to casualties, Government feared that the shipping companies would make Trincomalee their coaling station. It was already disadvantageous enough to have mail steamers call at Galle instead of Colombo. If the steamers called at Trincomalee rather than at Galle, the inconvenience would be very much greater.

So Government considered whether it would be possible to convert Galle harbour into a secure and sheltered anchorage throughout the year. On investigation it was found that the harbour could not be made sufficiently large, and that landing there could not be made safe enough during the south-west monsoon ; and that the expense involved was too heavy to be used on a place so far away from the centre of commerce.

On the other hand Government realized by this time the need for improving the Colombo roadstead. Unlike sailing vessels, steamers did not delay at the ports they touched, and they could not be sure of a quick departure from Colombo. If they were delayed unduly, they were bound to charge higher freights to make up for losses incurred through regular and over-long detention, and Ceylon would be at a disadvantage in competition with other producing countries. So Government decided to provide the steamers with an anchorage at Colombo which would afford them perfect shelter and safety all through the year. The result was that the commanding position of the harbour gave local trade a definite advantage over the trade of other competing countries, and Colombo became an important entrepôt for South India. In 1870, 78 steamers with a tonnage of 67,710 came to Colombo. In 1878 the number rose to 338 with a tonnage of 455,517. Colombo became the port of call for mail-steamers in 1882 and thus became a half-way house between London in the West and Australia, China and Japan in the East. From 1883 to 1889 the revenue of the harbour rose by 60 per cent. Trade expanded even more. The annual tonnage rose in 1890 to 5,117,902.

4. IRRIGATION WORKS AND THE PEASANTS

Gregory continued the restoration of irrigation works begun by Ward, but he and his successors did not show much concern about the return that accrued to Government from them. The chief aim of these restorations was to improve the condition of the peasants, especially to give those in very poor circumstances a chance of existing.

Gregory was specially struck by the pitiable state of the people of Nuvarakalāviya. The population of this district numbered about 60,000 persons. They occupied over 1,600 villages, each of which had a tank. But no tank had a sluice in working order, and so the peasants had to depend mainly on *chena* cultivation which led to the destruction of forests. Gregory repaired the Basavakkulam (Abhayaväva) in Anurādhapura and the Mahaväva at Mädavachchiya, and offered to construct free sluices for all village tanks the bunds of which the people repaired. The result was that under the energetic direction of the Government Agent Dickson the people, who were sunk in apathy and despair and were dying out through disease and lack of food, repaired some seven to eight hundred tanks in the hope of securing the advantages held out by Government. And the district, which earlier produced only 110,479 bushels of paddy, yielded 313,459 bushels in 1876.

Nuvarakalāviya, being in the Dry Zone far away from the mountains, could not get a constant supply of water from rain. So Gregory in his scheme for the improvement of the area planned the restoration of the Kalāväva and the Yōda Äla (the ancient Jaya Ganga) which connected the tank with the Tisāväva in Anurādhapura. Gordon continued these works in 1884 and completed them in 1887, providing the village tanks with an additional supply of water. He restored also the Älahära Canal, which traversed both the Central and the North-Central Provinces.

Gregory restored irrigation works in the Eastern Province also. He repaired the Kantalai Tank so that it might benefit the Trincomalee District in the way the Irakkāmam and Amparai Tanks benefited the Batticaloa District, and Gordon restored the Vēragoda Tank.

The improvement of the irrigation works in the Southern Province was also continued during this period. Gregory repaired the Ällavela Tank anicut. He completed the Tissamaharāma Tank begun by Robinson in 1871 and supplied it with water by building a dam across the Kirindi Oya. Gordon extended this scheme and restored the Valavē Ganga works and the Udukirivila works in the Tangalla District. Like the Kantalai Tank the Tissamaharāma Tank was repaired not so much to help the population around as to attract from other parts people sunk in poverty. Between 1881 and 1891 the population of this area more than doubled, rising from 473 to 1,016.

Another area in which the restoration of irrigation works was undertaken during this period was the North-Western Province. Gregory took in hand the repair of the Usväva and the Galgamuva Tank. Gordon restored works in the Vanni and the Demala Hatpattu. The value of the paddy crop in this district rose from Rs. 95,000 in 1880 to Rs. 241,470 in 1886.

Gordon extended the scheme for the restoration of irrigation works to the Ūva and the Sabaragamuva Provinces. In 1888 he began the restoration in Kongala Bintänna of the Hambegamuva Tank, which can be seen from Haputalē. This work was undertaken mainly for the improvement of the district and to assist the fever-stricken people of the place, most of whom suffered from parangi. Gordon had similar objects when he carried out the repair of the connected works extending from the Kitulbokka Āru to Tunkēma in Kolonna Kōralē. The people of this area did not know rice as an article of diet, and they suffered badly from parangi, fever, and other diseases.

Other steps were also taken to encourage the development of paddy cultivation. Reference has been made to the advances given to the peasants in the time of Robinson to undertake the repair of irrigation works. Gregory found that the terms governing the repayment of these advances discouraged landowners in many areas from undertaking such work, and he offered them the option of paying one rupee per acre to cover the cost of repair and maintenance. In the time of Longden a commission which reported on the grain tax condemned the system of farming by which it was collected. Gordon took a very keen interest in the cultivation of paddy. He regretted Government's neglect of irrigation in the past and stressed the view that nothing was more vital to the health, the comfort, and the very existence of the people than irrigation works. Fortunately for Gordon, at the time he governed Ceylon it was generally conceded in Britain that it was the duty of Government to attend to the welfare of its subjects, and in Ceylon one could see in many places the wonderful change that had been effected in villages which received an abundant supply of water. Consequently he was able to press on with his irrigation schemes. He spent three million rupees and repaired 42 tanks besides 164 sluices. In 1884 he established an Irrigation Board to consider the requirements for irrigation works. When this proved inadequate, he set up in 1887 Local Irrigation Boards in the provinces to sanction and direct the construction of smaller irrigation works, and in Colombo a Central Board with the Governor as president to deal with larger works. Moreover to prevent irrigation works from being neglected for want of money, he set aside one-fourth of the paddy tax as a contribution for their repairs.

The construction of irrigation works was not the only way in which the condition of the peasants was improved. Reference has been made to the steps taken to provide plantation areas with modern medical treatment. Gregory disapproved of the way the masses were neglected, especially as they were now prepared to avail themselves of Western treatment. To remedy the state of affairs, he followed the system of medical relief in Ireland, the country from which he come. He established small dispensaries in rural areas, and the medical officer in charge of the central hospital of the district attended these on certain days of the week.

5. ADMINISTRATIVE AND OTHER REFORMS

During this period Government maintained with no less vigour its policy of assisting the development of the resources of the country. Probably as a result of changes that were taking place in England, the Government of Ceylon took pains to improve the condition of the masses, who had received little attention since the Colebrooke reforms. These aims made Government reorganize the system of administration to some extent. It upset once more Colebrooke's division of Ceylon into five provinces, and the number of provinces was increased from six to nine. Other measures were adopted to raise the efficiency of Government and to improve the condition of the peasants.

Gregory created the North-Central Province in 1873. He found the Northern Province too large as an administrative unit. The Government Agent residing at Jaffna could not give the necessary attention to the remote district of Nuvarakalāviya, with the result that almost nothing had been done to improve this region or the miserable state of its people. He noticed further that the people of Nuvarakalāviya and of Tamankaduva (which belonged to the Eastern Province) had no natural connection with the Tamils who formed the rest of the inhabitants of the Northern and the Eastern Provinces. So he separated these districts and formed the new province with Anurādhapura as its capital.

In 1886 Gordon established the Province of Ūva with Badulla as its capital. It was formed by detaching Bintänna, Viyalūva, Vellassa, Udukinda and Yatikinda from the Central Province, and adding to them the Vällavāya and Buttala divisions of the Southern Province which were now connected by road with Badulla. The separation of Ūva was demanded both by the European planters and the Ceylonese upper classes as the Government Agent at Kandy was unable to supervise this remote district adequately. Owing to the plantations the Central Province had grown in importance and in population. In Uva too the number of plantations in the Badulla, Madulsīma, Monerāgala and Välimada areas had increased and was expected to rise still further with the extension of the railway. The villages of this area needed more attention as their population was diminishing owing to droughts and the neglect of irrigation works.

The third province created was Sabaragamuva. Gordon discovered that both the Kāgalla and the Ratnapura district had decreased in wealth, and the latter in population as well. The Government Agent of the Western Province, unable to give sufficient attention to the remote districts of his area, had spent no money on roads, schools, rest-houses, or irrigation works in the Kukulu Kōralē. To remedy this state of affairs, in 1889 the Kāgalla and the Ratnapura districts were separated from the Western Province, and formed into a new province with Ratnapura as its capital.

The expansion of administrative work also led to the establishment of Assistant Agencies at Mātalē, Kalutara, Negombo and Chilaw. The Mātalē District had grown more important owing to the increase in plantations, and Mātalē had become a centre of trade. The population of the Western Province increased from 554,000 to 776,000 between 1846 and 1874, and in 1875 Assistant Agents were stationed at Kalutara and Negombo. Within two years of the establishment of the kachcheri at Negombo, the revenue of the district rose by a third.

In 1888 the district of Chilaw was separated from that of Puttalam. During the previous decade a large number of coconut plantations had been opened in this area and the population had increased. The seat of the Assistant Agent would have been transferred to Chilaw had not the interests of Government in the large salt revenue of Puttalam demanded vigilant supervision.

When Gregory established the Assistant Agency at Mātalē, he also had in view the development of the area around Dambulla which was suitable for the cultivation of rice. For a similar reason he appointed an Assistant Agent at Vavuniya-Vilankulam which lay on the border of the North-Central Province. In 1888 this region was amalgamated with Mullaitīvu, and from 1889 it was called the Vavuniya District.

The needs of Government and of the people had gradually led to the establishment of a number of departments, and at the beginning of this period there were the Departments of Public Works, of the Surveyor General, of Public Instruction, of the Royal Botanic Gardens, and the Medical, Police, Postal, Railway, Harbour, Customs and Registration (Registrar General's) Departments. Their work was co-ordinated not only at headquarters but where possible in every province as well. The people of the rural areas were fit only for a paternal form of government and could not appreciate a purely bureaucratic system. Hence the Government Agents were expected to co-ordinate the work of the different departments within their districts and to see that their officers served the interests of the people. They not only maintained order and collected revenue but also took an interest in the improvement of roads and communications, the restoration of irrigation works, the settlement of land disputes, the development of plantations and paddy-cultivation, the construction of public works, the maintenance of forests, and in all other matters affecting the district.

The headman system continued during this period with no important change. Government realized that the time was not yet ripe to extend a bureaucratic system any further into the villages. Such an extension would not only have led to friction between villagers and government officers but also would have set up against Government the important families in the rural areas from which headmen were recruited.

In the time of Gregory some officials objected to the appointments of chief headmen in the Kandyan provinces being limited to members of the old aristocratic families. The Civil Service had been opened to competition, and many persons who belonged to the middle class had entered the Service. Progressive officials saw no objection to the selection of headmen also from among well-trained men who had risen from the ranks. Such appointments, however, proved a failure as the Kandyans were bound by caste and attached much importance to birth. Nevertheless by the end of this period Government was of opinion that the headman system, the methods of which were medieval, could not last much longer against modern influences and the process of centralizing which Government was pursuing

Conditions in the prisons were also improved. At this time all prisoners were herded together at night, the worst criminals with those convicted for trivial offences. Gregory disapproved of this, and with the object of giving a separate cell at night to every prisoner, the existing jails were improved and five new ones built.

Further judicial and legal reforms took place during this period. When the British came to Ceylon they found that though Sinhalese and Tamil laws were well developed in certain matters such as family relations, they were deficient in other respects. There was no law of procedure, criminal or civil, no law of torts, no public or constitutional law, and the law of contract was inadequate to satisfy modern requirements. When Ceylon under British rule began to emerge from a feudal into a commercial state, new laws were required to suit new needs. The Dutch had ruled the Sinhalese and the Tamils according to their own laws, but they had applied Roman-Dutch Law whenever the Sinhalese and Tamil laws proved inadequate. In 1799 North had guaranteed the continuance of Roman-Dutch Law, and as time passed it began to be applied in an increasing degree and gradually became the common law of the land.

But Roman-Dutch Law, which did not provide for the new commercial developments, proved unsatisfactory in another respect. Dutch penal laws, like those of all other countries in Europe, grew out of date with the changes made as a result of the humanitarian movement. In 1861 a new Penal Code came into force in India. When it was drafted in 1854, it was considered above the level of English criminal law at the time. In 1885 the criminal law of Ceylon based on Roman-Dutch Law was repealed and a new Penal Code, largely composed of transcripts and adaptations of the Indian Penal Code, was adopted. The procedure of the courts too was regulated by a Criminal Procedure Code based on the Indian Code of Criminal Procedure. The new Penal Code raised the powers of punishment of the District and Police Courts in order to relieve the Supreme Court of a part of its work. It also reduced the number of persons who formed a jury to nine, and this was later brought down to seven.

The interest taken by Government during this period in backward communities led to an increase in the number of unofficial members in the Legislative Council. In 1889 two unofficial members were added to represent the Kandyans and the Moors. The Kandyans had been affected little by European influences before the British occupation, and even after 1815 new ideas had permeated Kandyan society very slowly. Though plantations were established mainly within their territory, the Kandyans hardly took to trade or to the other activities that followed in its train. Christian missionaries had not shown the same interest in spreading education among them as they had done in the Maritime Provinces. Though some Muslims undoubtedly benefited by the new opportunities for trade afforded by British rule, as a community they made little progress; for their religious beliefs and their social conservatism discouraged them from studying in Mission schools.

The military vote, which created so much friction between Government and the unofficials, came up once more when the revenue fell owing to the coffee disease. The Ceylon Government asked for its reduction, and the Imperial Government, which had lowered it in 1873 to £124,000, on the disbandment of the Ceylon Rifles reduced it to Rs. 600,000 in 1885.

The Municipal Ordinance of 1865, referred to in the last chapter, was amended in 1886 to raise the efficiency of the Councils. The amendments gave the councils additional powers to control the sanitation of their towns. They raised the property qualification of the municipal electors and gave greater responsibility to the executive. Hitherto those who broke the bye-laws of the Municipality were punished by the councillors themselves. The new ordinance transferred these judicial duties to a magistrate.

In 1889 Colombo was provided with a supply of drinking water. In the latter part of the nineteenth century people in England began to realize that diseases were due mainly to bacteria and that one of the chief sources of infection was impure water. Well-water was satisfactory in villages, but in towns it easily became impure owing to cess-pits. Hence steps began to be taken to obtain water for towns from outside. The idea of giving Colombo a pure supply of water was mooted in the time of Robinson, and the construction of the Labugama Reservoir, from which water was conveyed to Colombo in pipes, was completed in the time of Gordon.

In 1876 a Local Board of Health and Improvement Bill was passed to promote sanitation and small works of utility in towns not advanced enough to have municipalities. The Boards established by the ordinance consisted of three elected members and three members nominated by the Governor, with the Government Agent or his Assistant as chairman. They were empowered to frame bye-laws, levy rates, and regulate matters pertaining to streets, lights and markets. The powers hitherto vested in the Boards of Health and in the Provincial and District Committees which looked after branch roads and rest-houses were transferred to them.

6. EDUCATION

In the seventies and eighties the Department of Public Instruction continued to carry out the recommendations of the Education Committee, and the number of schools increased rapidly. In 1872 there were 200 Government schools with 10,852 pupils, and 402 Grant-in-aid schools with 25,443 pupils. At the close of this period in 1890 there were 436 Government schools with 40,290 pupils, and 984 Grant-in-aid schools with 73,698 pupils. Thus the number of schools more than doubled and the number of pupils more than trebled during these eighteen years. The percentage of literacy among males rose from 24·6 in 1881 to 27·9 in 1891, and that of females from 2·5 to 4·4. The increase would have been greater but for the fall of revenue from 1881 owing to the coffee disease. During the decade from 1892 the Government schools increased only by 7·6 per cent., and the Grant-in-aid schools, whose grants were reduced from year to year from 1885, by 23 per cent. Most of the schools opened during this period were vernacular schools. The Missions added to their number chiefly in the Maritime Provinces, while the Government set up schools mainly in the interior, especially in the Central, North-Central and North-Western Provinces.

At this time Government lost its interest in English schools, which had been its chief concern since 1832. In 1873 English education was mainly in its hands, and there were English or Anglo-vernacular schools in all district capitals except in the north. But from 1881 with the fall in revenue Government began either to close down its English and Anglo-vernacular schools or to hand them over to the Missionary bodies.

But the number of English schools actually rose. With the expansion of government activities and the economic development of the country, the need for English schools increased, and the

Christian Missions and other bodies met the demand, taking advantage of the grants-in-aid given by Government. When the Government Anglo-vernacular schools were abolished in 1889, Grant-in-aid schools held almost the entire field of English education.

The pol cy of connecting English education in Ceylon with that of England rather than that of India was maintained during this period. In 1880 the Cambridge examinations were introduced into Ceylon. Their adoption by English schools was encouraged by awarding the university scholarships on the results of the Cambridge Senior Examination, and by throwing the scholarships open to general competition instead of confining them as hitherto to the pupils of the Colombo Academy. Twenty-one candidates took these examinations in 1880, and in 1890 the number rose to 223.

In spite of these changes the standard of education imparted in the schools continued to be poor. The importance of training teachers, which was emphasised by the 1867 Committee, was lost sight of before many years passed. The Normal School, meant to provide teachers for Government schools, gradually disappeared. The English class failed to attract the right type of students and was abolished in 1881. The same fate befell the Anglo-vernacular class in 1883. The vernacular department was closed in 1886 and was replaced by smaller establishment in Colombo, Kandy and Galle, the advantages gained from a central institution thus being lost.

The development of the country and the gradual expansion of the legal profession led to changes in legal education. Since 1833 advocates and proctors had been admitted and enrolled by the judges of the Supreme Court after an examination. In 1873 the Council of Legal Education was established to direct the studies of advocate students. Henceforth all students were required to pass a preliminary examination, attend lectures provided by the Council, and pass another examination at the end of their course. The training of proctor students was confined to their course of apprenticeship till 1889, when they too were in addition required to follow a similar course of studies and examinations before they were enrolled as proctors.

7. BUDDHISM AND HINDUISM

Buddhist activities made great headway during this time. In 1873 there was at Pānadurē another public controversy between Protestant Christians and Buddhists. Thousands of Buddhists assembled to hear the discussion and showed their great interest in their religion and their anxiety about its future. The chief figure at this controversy was Migettuvattē Gunānanda, who had taken part in some of the previous controversies. By his oratory he exercised an immense influence over the minds of his hearers and gave strength to the cause of Buddhism.

The controversy ended peacefully but had far-reaching effects. Discussions with regard to the merits and defects of Buddhism and Christianity continued in the Sinhalese journals run by Buddhists, Roman Catholics and Protestants. An account of the controversy reached Colonel Olcott, who was to play an important part in the history of Ceylon Buddhism. At this time with advances in scientific studies there was much interest among the educated classes in Europe and America in the religions and institutions of other races. In New York in 1875 the Russian, Madame Blavatsky, and the American, H. S. Olcott, founded the Theosophical Society, with the discovery of truth in all religions as one of its objects. In 1878 they made Adyar in Madras their headquarters and began the study of Hinduism. In 1880 Olcott came to Ceylon and adopted Buddhism. He and his Western followers championed Buddhist aims and practices, idealized Ceylon's past, and placed Buddhism on a higher plane than Christianity, which they opposed as an exotic religion. Their influence definitely encouraged the revival of Buddhism, which the Christian missionaries had helped to discredit.

Olcott realized that Buddhist activities needed to be organized on modern lines. In 1880 the Buddhist Theosophical Society was formed in order to establish Buddhist schools, and a sum over a thousand rupees was raised at the inaugural meeting. At the end of the year the Sinhalese newspaper *Sarasavi Sandaräsa* was started to carry on Buddhist propaganda, and an English supplement called *The Buddhist* was added to it. In 1885 a building was purchased for the headquarters of the Society. A Buddhist flag was adopted and Government was asked to make Vesak (the birthday of the Buddha) a public holiday. Buddhist Sunday schools were started; in 1886 one of them was converted into an English day school which finally developed into the present Ānanda College. A number of other schools were also opened, and in 1890 they numbered nearly fifty.

Their zeal for new organizations did not prevent the Buddhists from developing their ancient institutions. In the ancient days these were established and maintained by kings and chiefs. That work was now undertaken by members of the new middle class who had acquired wealth by taking to new enterprises. Reference has been made to the pirivena established at Ratmalāna. In 1873 the Vidyōdaya Pirivena was started at Māligākanda in Colombo with the learned scholar Hikkaduvē Srī Sumangala as its principal. In 1876 the Vidyālankāra Pirivena was established at Pāliyagoda in Kälaniya with Ratmalanē Srī Dharmāloka as its principal.

This revival of Buddhism gave a new impetus to oriental studies. Early in the nineteenth century Christian missionaries and Civil Servants had begun the study of Pāli and Sinhalese assisted by Buddhist scholars. They had compiled dictionaries and produced works on Buddhism and Hinduism. George Turnour had published in 1837, together with an English translation, the first part of the *Mahāvansa*, the ancient chronicle of Ceylon from its legendary beginnings to A.D. 362. The branch of the Royal Asiatic Society founded in 1845 had begun to investigate the ancient heritage of Ceylon. In 1852 James de Alwis had published an edition of the *Sidat Sangarāva*, the Sinhalese grammar written in the thirteenth century, besides other Pāli and Sinhalese works. Gregory established the Colombo Museum in 1876. The scholars who passed out of the Ratmalāna Pirivena began to edit and publish Sanskrit, Pāli and Sinhalese works, and helped the study of these languages in the country.

Similar developments took place in the north. Some Hindus who had been educated in Christian schools and had acquired wealth in the employ of Government and in other ways started in 1888 the Saiva Paripālana Sabhai (Society for the Propagation of Saivism). They were inspired partly by Arumuka Nāvalar, who continued to work for a religious and literary revival until his death in 1879 and partly by the Hindu revival in India caused by the joint efforts of the Brahmo Samaj, the Ārya Samaj, Rāmakrishna Paramhamsa and the Theosophical Society. The Sabhai tried to check proselytism by the Christian Missions and to spread Hinduism. Realizing the power of the press, it started in 1889 the *Hindu Organ*, an English and Tamil fortnightly; and it held conferences, arranged for public lectures, and published text-books, pamphlets and tracts. Education up to this time had been almost a monopoly of the Missions, and had been the chief means of conversion to Christianity. So the Sabhai began to concentrate on education. In 1890 it took over the Town High School which under its management developed later into the Jaffna Hindu College.

It has been seen how the arrangements made in 1853 for the management of the Buddhist temporalities failed. In 1876 Gregory, who received numerous complaints about the misuse of vihāra and dēvāla properties, appointed a Commission consisting of the Government Agents of the Western, Central and the North-Western Provinces and three Buddhists to inquire into the way in which these properties were administered. The Commission unanimously reported on 'the necessity for the intervention of Government to put a stop to the scandalous misappropriation of the temple revenues and widespread corruption and systematic fraud disclosed by the evidence'. Acting on its recommendations, Gregory in 1877 proposed to vest the control of Buddhist temporalities in three Commissioners appointed by the Governor. But the Secretary of State objected again to any interference by Government, and suggested the establishment of Boards of Management, each with an official member who might act as a check on others. At this time the Church of England, the Church of Scotland, and the Dutch Presbyterian Church, whose clergy hitherto were appointed by Government and paid from public revenues, were disestablished and Longden did not approve of this interference; and the next Secretary of State, Kimberley, agreeing with him, suggested the establishment of an organisation such as the churches enjoyed. He probably did not realize that such an institution would be too complicated for the Kandyan Buddhists to manage. Ultimately nothing was done and grave and scandalous abuses continued to disgrace the administration of dēvāla and vihāra properties.

In 1886 Gordon examined the question again, but found that he could not devise a satisfactory scheme to be worked unaided by Government. As he had to do something, he passed an ordinance in 1889 based on the principles enunciated by Longden and the Secretaries of State, Kimberley and Derby, and transferred the control of Buddhist properties in each district to a committee of Buddhist laymen elected by the Buddhist bhikshus and laymen of the area, empowering it to elect the trustees of the vihārēs and the dēvālēs in the district. In addition a Provincial Committee was appointed to act as a check on these district committees. Such an arrangement might have worked well with an educated community, but at that time the Kandyans could not make it succeed. Like the arrangement of 1853, it failed, and dēvāla and vihāra properties continued to suffer from neglect and the misappropriation of their wealth.

PART III

FROM CROWN COLONY TO FULL RESPONSIBLE GOVERNMENT

CHAPTER IX

THE REORGANIZATION OF GOVERNMENT AND THE REFORM OF THE LEGISLATURE (1891-1913)

1. ADMINISTRATIVE REFORMS

The Government of Ceylon during this period followed the lines of advance already laid down. It continued to assist the development of plantations. It constructed roads, railways, and telegraphs, and restored irrigation works. It attended to the health of the people and helped to spread education among them. It did more: the system of government was carefully overhauled. Department after department was reorganized and new ones were created. The process of centralization was quickened, administrative methods were modified, and the whole system of government was made more efficient.

The establishment of departments had no doubt begun at the commencement of British rule, and the Departments of the Surveyor-General, the Civil Engineer, the Royal Botanic Gardens, the Land Registry, and the Department of Public Instruction, besides the Medical, Postal, and other Departments had come into existence. But with the exception of the Departments of Public Works and of the Surveyor-General, none of these yet played an important part in the administration of the island as a whole.

At this time governments in the West revised the aims, widened the scope, and modified the methods of their systems of administration. Scientific developments enabled, and industrial competition demanded greater efficiency in government and the provision of wider amenities for the working classes whose standards of living had to be raised. British officials deriving their inspiration for administrative changes from Britain attempted similar reforms in India. Curzon (1898-1905) reorganized the administration and converted 'a practically unchallenged bureaucracy into something closely resembling a benevolent autocracy'. Ceylon too had the prerequisities for such changes. A network of roads covered many parts of the island; the railway connected the most important areas; the telegraph linked the centres of the administration; and English schools provided men qualified to fill posts in the lower branches of the administrative and technical services. There was also the money needed: Ceylon was never more prosperous. The revenue which had risen to Rs. 17,960,710 in 1891 went up to the extraordinary figure of Rs. 43,471,738 in 1912. The total trade which had grown to Rs. 117,342,259 in 1891 rose to Rs. 346,434,756 in 1912. Further loans for productive schemes were easily procurable from the accumulated savings of the British people. And Sir West Ridgeway (1896-1903) and his successors gave an impetus to such changes in Ceylon.

The general reorganization did not lead to radical changes in the Civil Service, the steel frame which held the government together, but showed that it had some defects which needed attention. The Civil Servant no longer concerned himself merely with the collection of revenue, the maintenance of peace and order, the manual of instructions of the Central Government, and the needs of the peasants. He had also to provide for the more exacting demands of the middle class in the towns and supervise the activities of the numerous technical officers who encroached on his rights. On the whole the standard of the Civil Service had been maintained since the sixties. In 1878 salaries had been raised to meet the increased cost of living and the depreciation of the rupee. But, so that no one might suffer in the matter of emoluments, one practice which affected the efficiency of the Service had been allowed to continue. At this time salaries were attached to posts and not to persons, and whenever a vacancy occurred in one of the higher grades, a number of promotions were made without sufficient regard to the fitness of the persons for the posts. With the growing complexity of government, the evils of frequent transfers and the unsuitability of some Civil Servants for certain posts became more apparent.

To put an end to these administrative defects, Ridgeway introduced in 1897 an incremental scale of salaries, attaching the salary, except in special cases, to the individual, and making the appointments in the second and the third grades, and in the fourth and the fifth grades of the Service, interchangeable. From this time it became possible to make appointments according to the fitness of the officer, and to keep him in a post for a long period whenever necessary without harming his prospects.

Quite a different reason led to a modification of the rules of admission to the Civil Service. Reference has been made to Colebrooke's recommendations regarding the employment of Ceylonese in the Civil Service. But Ceylonese had found it difficult to enter the Service owing to the qualifications imposed in order to raise its efficiency in 1845. From 1870 the examination for admission to the Civil Service had been held simultaneously in England and in Ceylon to enable Ceylonese to enter it without making a voyage to England. But this made no difference as provision was not made at the same time to enable them to acquire the education which the Civil Service examination demanded since 1857, and the holding of the examination had been adandoned in 1880. The absence of an institution which gave advanced technical education prevented them also from obtaining higher appointments in the technical departments. Government at this time made almost a cult of efficiency, and preferred to obtain officers from the British Isles to uphold its standards and probably to maintain its power as well. The British officers now formed a ruling caste and did not favour the appointment of Ceylonese to the higher posts. But the standard of education in Ceylon had risen since 1880, and the better educated members of the Ceylonese middle class, no longer satisfied with posts in the lowest grades, demanded opportunities for entering the Civil Service and the technical departments. Sir Henry McCallum (1907-1913) made a few concessions to allay this growing discontent. He changed the Lower Division of the Civil Service, hitherto manned by those promoted from the Clerical Service, into the Local Division. The number of posts in the Local Division was almost doubled and the appointments to it were made through a competitive test. At the same time promotion into the Civil Service was made possible for efficient Clerical Servants at the top of their Service. McCallum also proposed to create a similar local division in the Public Works Department. The efficiency of the Clerical Service too was raised about the same time. It was divided into four classes and its members were granted an incremental scale of salaries, promotions being made dependent on merit in addition to seniority. The Survey, Postal and Telegraph, and the Railway Departments whose officers were not transferable to other departments, were also similarly reorganized.

The zeal for administrative reform affected even more the methods of rural government. The provincial system of administration had come into being when most parts of the country were difficult of access, and the activities of Government were of a negative character. The Government Agents then ruled the districts according to their discretion, with the help of their Assistants and the old hierarchy of officials—Mudaliyars, Ratēmahatmayas or Maniagārs, Muhandirams, Kōralas or Udaiyars, and Vidanes or Ārachchis. At first this system met the requirements of the people, but when Government began to expand its activities and assume the positive functions of a modern state, it ceased to satisfy both the Central Government and the educated public. So some of its duties were gradually handed over to the various departments. But administration by departments did not suit the peasants who could not appreciate such institutions. As they were still backward and required a paternal form of government, in the provinces Government Agents were left in charge of all matters which directly affected them. McCallum took a further step to improve the conditions in the rural areas. In the seventies Gregory had started annual conferences of Government Agents to enable them to place before him their proposals for the improvement of their districts. McCallum revived the durbars of chiefs in order to consult them on rural problems. He probably was more hopeful of the continued usefulness of Sinhalese and Tamil chiefs as officials than Gordon, who feared that they would be an anachronism in a modern system of government. In India too at this time the British Government changed its attitude towards the Indian Princes and began to rely on them more and more in the face of the opposition to its rule by the rebellious sections of the growing middle class.

The failure of the Provincial Administration to maintain order by suppressing crime was the chief cause of the reorganization of the Police Department. In the provinces this work fell to the Government Agents and their Assistants, who performed it through the police in the urban areas and the headmen in the rural districts. As Robert Knox's *Historical Relation of Ceylon* shows, crime does not appear to have been common under the Sinhalese kings. Even in the earlier days of British rule it was such as could be tackled by the headmen. But crime increased with the development of communications, the disintegration of the old social system, and the rise of disputes over property. In the villages headmen often found it beyond their power to prevent breaches of the peace; in urban areas the police failed equally badly. Influenced probably by British administrative practice, the responsibility of the Inspector-General of Police was limited at this time to the Colombo Division. Outside this area his duty was only to report on the efficiency of the Police Force. Government Agents who were in charge of it were too burdened with diverse duties to give sufficient attention to its discipline and training.

Ridgeway adopted various measures to reduce crime. Finding these inadequate, Sir Henry Blake (1903-1907) decided that what was needed was a reform of the Police Force. He improved the pay and conditions of service in order to attract a better type of officers and men. To keep the connection with the Provincial Administration, he appointed Civil Servants as Superintendents and Assistant Superintendents of the Force, and made the Inspector-General of Police responsible for its efficiency and discipline. He extended the control of the police to the rural districts of the Western, the Southern, and a part of the North-Western Provinces, so that the police might be of assistance to the headmen in suppressing crime.

McCallum carried out further reforms. He felt that police officers required a special training which could not be acquired by Civil Servants who had various other duties to perform. So he began to fill the higher posts, to which Civil Servants were hitherto appointed, with candidates who were successful at the examination for recruitment to the Indian Police.

Another department which encroached on the duties of Government Agents was the Department of Irrigation. At first a special and separate staff of the Public Works Department had carried out the restoration of irrigation works in co-operation with the Government Agents, but it had gradually died out in the time of Longden. Government had a definite policy with regard to the development of plantations and communications. Gordon wanted to give stability and continuity to Government's irrigation policy too. In order to achieve these objects he established a Central Irrigation Board and Provincial Irrigation Boards. But these Boards did not prove a success. The members of the Provincial Boards included the Government Agent, the Chief Surveyor, and the Provincial Engineer; but as their personnel constantly changed, the Boards not only failed to maintain a continuous policy, but also made recommendations which when carried out did not produce the expected results. The work of restoration was no longer performed in the ancient way, but according to modern scientific methods which demanded a technical knowledge from the chief officers who undertook the work. The Boards had not their own officers and entrusted the work to the Departments of Public Works and of the Surveyor-General. But both these departments were busy and could not give adequate attention to irrigation. Moreover the Central Board had not the expert knowledge to judge the relative merits of the proposals submitted by the Provincial Boards, and often decided in favour of those which were not the most useful or the most urgent. To remove these drawbacks, Ridgeway in 1898 revived the Irrigation Department as a branch of the Public Works Department, with Henry Parker[1] as Irrigation Assistant. Henceforth irrigation works did not have to wait the convenience of the Departments of Public Works and of the Surveyor-General, while the Central Board had the service of an expert to advise on the utility and the relative merits of the recommendations made by the Provincial Boards. In 1900 five million rupees were set apart for the development of irrigation, and the works involved justified an increased staff and the creation of a separate department. Ridgeway took this opportunity to make the Irrigation Department independent. The Provincial Boards were abolished the following year and their advisory duties transferred to the Government Agents. In 1906 Blake abolished the Central Board as it was unwieldy for efficient work and its existence took away much of the responsibility of the Director. Thus the Irrigation Department was placed on the same basis as the other departments.

These steps undoubtedly led to greater administrative efficiency, but they did not always serve the interests of the peasants. The village works were carried out at this time by them, under the supervision of the Government Agents with the technical advice and assistance of the Department. But in the case of the larger irrigation works the Department not only regulated and distributed the water, but also made itself responsible for the purely agricultural part of paddy cultivation under it. McCallum did not approve of this as it removed the direct interest of the Government Agents, who were likely to understand the needs of the people better, in an important activity, and he limited the work of the Department even in major works to irrigation alone.

Forests too were at first entirely within the purview of Government Agents. Since the British occupation many forests had been destroyed for the opening of plantations; others had been damaged by the indiscriminate felling of trees for timber and by *chēna*

1 Henry Parker is the author of *Ancient Ceylon*, a book giving a great deal of information on the ancient Sinhalese civilization.

cultivation. The preservation and the re-cultivation of forests required a technical knowledge which the Government Agents did not possess, and the establishment of the Forest Department in 1889 had placed the more valuable forests under the Conservator of Forests. But partly owing to the dual control of the Government Agents and the Conservator of Forests there was little progress in the reservation of forests, the demarcation of forest areas, the blocking out of areas for planting, and the measuring and marking of mature trees. Therefore in 1899 the respective spheres of the Government Agents and of the Forest Officers were defined and the Department was reorganized. In the time of McCallum, in order to take further advantage of the advances made in the science of forestry, the higher posts in the Department were reserved for officers trained in Britain and on the continent of Europe, while the posts of Rangers were given to those trained in India.

Scientific advance in Europe enabled, and administrative needs in Ceylon contributed to the reorganization of the Survey Department. The Department had been established by North as early as 1800 in connection with his land reforms. It played an important part in the development of plantations by surveying all land for sale. It did a great amount of work in tracing the roads that were to be built to open up the plantation areas too, and was responsible for their construction as well until in 1846 the Public Works Department was constituted as a separate department. But it did hardly any other work in the nineteenth century. The result was that that at the beginning of the century the available maps of Ceylon were so full of errors that they failed to serve the needs of a modern government. Besides Government had continuous disputes regarding title of lands and could not settle them without a detailed survey. To meet these requirements Ridgeway enlarged the scope of the Department and in 1897 commenced the Topographical and the Cadastral or Block Surveys. The object of the first was to produce an accurate map of the island on the scale of an inch to a mile, and that of the latter was to demarcate definitely and to map all crown lands in order to settle disputes between Government and private owners of land. Before the end of McCallum's rule contour surveys extending over 1,000 square miles, and surveys of the North-Western and the Central Provinces, 5,300 square miles in extent, were carried out.

To complete his work Ridgeway established in 1903 the Land Settlement Department to ensure the speedy settlement of titles to the vast tracts of waste land. He realized that the work required specialized knowledge and could not be dealt with adequately or quickly enough by busy Government Agents.

The passing of the Waste Lands Ordinance considerably increased the work of the Registrar-General's Department. For instance, the average number of title deeds registered in the time of Ridgeway was fifty per cent. more than in the time of Havelock (1890-1895). The necessity of statistics and the registration of all births, marriages and deaths was better realized at the time. This led to an expansion of the staff, the adoption of more efficient methods of registration, and the general reorganization of the Department.

Scientific advance in Europe enabled the reorganization of the Department of Royal Botanic Gardens too. This Department too had its beginnings in the time of North. It had conducted botanical and horticultural work at Pērādeniya and the branch gardens at Hakgala, Henaratgoda, Anurādhapura and Badulla, and had introduced into Ceylon useful and ornamental plants from other countries. Reference has been made to the valuable services it rendered in the introduction and diffusion of such plants as tea, cinchona and cocoa. But it did little research on plant diseases or methods of cultivation, and planters received hardly any technical advice from it on the difficulties they had to face.

In 1896 the Department of the Royal Botanic Gardens widened the scope of its work. It began systematic research in matters connected with tropical agriculture, especially in products likely to be of commercial value In 1897 it started the *Agricultural Journal* to diffuse scientific knowledge on agricultural subjects. In 1899 it established a botanical laboratory, and in 1901 purchased Gannoruva Estate for use as an experiment station. In 1902 it extended its range further by the addition of several scientific experts to its staff, and developed into a department of scientific tropical agriculture and a bureau of information and advice on questions relating to botany, agriculture, horticulture, entomology, and plant pathology and chemistry. In 1912 it was further reorganized and enlarged, and its name was changed into the Department of Agriculture

The Department of Royal Botanic Gardens was of great assistance to the major agricultural industries. It showed tea planters how to improve their methods of cultivation and manufacture and saved both tea and coconuts from pests. During the years 1897 to 1899 it carried out various experiments in rubber, and discovered better methods of securing rubber and preparing it for the market. It showed how the yield of latex could be increased and how trees can be tapped within six or seven years of the time of planting. In these and in other ways it helped to revolutionize the rubber industry.

But it did little to improve the methods of peasant agriculture. The chief means it adopted to help peasants was to establish school gardens. Following the example of Curzon in India, in 1911 McCallum established Co-operative Credit Societies. Their object was to provide peasants with credit at reasonable rates of interest, to reduce indebtedness and to develop self-help, thrift and co-operation. But this was very little compared with what was done for the major industries.

Reference has already been made to the new interest shown in Oriental studies, which had led to the establishment of the Colombo Museum in 1876. In 1890 an Archaeological Department was set up, and an Antiquities Ordinance was passed in 1900 to provide for and facilitate the preservation of the numerous historical remains.

Scientific development also led to the establishment of three other departments. The income of the Government from pearl fisheries had been precarious and sometimes amounted to little for long periods. The advances made in practical biology in Europe led Ridgeway to appoint an expert to inquire into the pearl fisheries as well as the economic potentialities of the surrounding sea in regard to other marine creatures. The investigations proved valuable and led to the establishment of the Department of Marine Biology

About the same time it was proposed to carry out a geological survey to develop the latent resources of the island, but Government failed to obtain a suitable officer for this purpose. Thereupon it was decided to carry out a mineralogical survey of the island instead, and Dr. Ananda K. Coomaraswamy was given charge of the work.

Another problem that had engaged the attention of Government for a long time was cattle diseases, among them rinderpest, which disorganized paddy cultivation as well as transport. From 1865 to 1867 the deaths of cattle by disease each year had amounted to ten per cent. of their total number, causing an annual loss of £60,000. To deal with these diseases Government appointed a Veterinary Surgeon, and attached him at first to the Department of

Public Instruction. As this arrangement failed, a separate department was established, and its work was carried out in co-operation with the provincial administrative officers.

Reference has been made to Government's interest in the sale of arrack. Government had to deal at this time with its manufacture and distribution. For their supervision and control a system of excise similar to that in Madras was introduced in 1909, and the work involved necessitated the establishment of the Excise Department.

The development of the country and the growth of prosperity led to a great expansion of the Postal Department, while the extension of the roads and railways and the introduction of motor vehicles made a quicker and more efficient service possible. The work of the Postal Department had increased considerably since 1877, and between 1890 and 1913 its expansion surpassed all previous records.[1]

The Public Works Department was also reorganized at this time. Reference has been made to its origin as the Department of the Civil Engineer and its growth into the Public Works Department. The Department at first concerned itself mainly with trunk roads, and gradually began to help the plantations by the construction of branch roads. In 1848 when every male inhabitant was required to work six days a year in the construction and the repair of roads or pay instead a commutation tax, Provincial and District Committees were established to deal with minor roads. But with the development of the country many of these became trunk roads and had to be handed over to the Public Works Department. During this period a considerable number of such roads was taken over, and together with the construction of new ones, work expanded greatly and the staff of the Department had to be greatly increased.

1 For instance in the time of Ridgeway the weight of mails doubled, parcels increased by 60 per cent., the number of money orders rose by 90 per cent. and their value by 70 per cent., the deposits in the Post Office Savings Bank increased by 80 per cent. and the amount to the credit of the depositors by 73 per cent. The number of letters to foreign countries also increased during this period. In 1893 the rate for letters to foreign countries was reduced to 15 cents, and in 1898 to a penny to empire countries. The number of post offices and receiving offices rose from 139 and 148 in 1895 to 149 and 190 in 1903. In Blake's time the number of post offices went up to 156. The revenue rose from Rs. 1,091,000 in 1903 to Rs. 1,249,000 in 1906.

Government's interest in plantations and in health greatly increased the activities of the Medical Department. Hospitals and dispensaries were built in every province.[1] They were mainly intended to provide treatment to labourers on the plantations and to peasants in rural areas. Those built in rural areas were mostly in regions where irrigation was being developed, or in towns and villages situated near important junctions of roads.

Steps were taken also to make medical and surgical work conform to the latest developments in science. In 1899 the Bacteriological and Pasteuer Institute was established, and in 1905 a clinic for tropical diseases. Another asylum for lepers was established at Māntai near Mannār, and the number of infectious diseases hospitals was increased. In the time of Ridgeway the Lady Havelock Hospital for women and children was established, and in the time of McCallum a campaign was started to combat tuberculosis.

With the expansion of its work the Department of Public Instruction also had to make adjustments in its machinery. The majority of the schools at this time were run not by Government but by Christian Missions. These Missions had been represented on the School Commission; but now with no voice in the policy of the Department, they often found themselves in conflict with it. In 1905 the relations between the Department and the Missions became very strained, and to create a better understanding Government established the Board of Education, consisting of officers of the Department and representatives of the Missions.

It has been pointed out how humanitarian motives led to reforms in the system of prison administration. Further steps were taken during this period to improve the conditions in prisons. One officer had been in charge of the Police and of the Prisons. In 1905 the post of Inspector-General of Police was separated from that of the Inspector-General of Prisons for the greater efficiency of both departments. The policy of closing the smaller jails scattered throughout the country was continued as the prisoners did not receive proper attention in them. The Maggona Reformatory was opened for all young offenders, who before that time were sent to the same prisons as adult criminals. The inmates at Maggona were taught useful occupations which would enable them to earn a living after their term of imprisonment. In McCallum's

1 317 hospitals and dispensaries treated 794,700 patients in 1895. 64 hospitals and 467 dispensaries treated 1,041,615 patients in 1902, and 66 hospitals and 502 dispensaries treated 1,531,138 patients in 1906. In 1913 there were 75 hospitals and 511 dispensaries.

time older criminals were also given the chance of learning crafts such as cloth-weaving and printing.

Reference has been made in previous chapters to the various steps taken to reform the system of law that prevailed in Ceylon. A few important changes were made during this period too. The process of bringing the laws of Ceylon into line with those of England was continued. At this time English law was applied in almost all matters of commerce; but as there was no specific ordinance dealing with the sale of goods, some judges followed the Roman-Dutch Law in such cases. So an ordinance was passed in 1896 to make the law clear on this point. In the following year the banking companies were allowed as in England to be incorporated under the Joint Stock Companies' Ordinance.

In Havelock's time steps were taken to consolidate and amend the law of evidence. At the time there was no specific ordinance to guide judges on the subject, and they had to consult English text-books and reports of legal decisions.

Undivided shares of property, a cause of much crime, was one of the problems which demanded immediate solution. This matter had received some consideration even from the first governor North on economic grounds. But Government paid little attention to the problem. All it did was to encourage people to divide their shares by exempting in 1897 all partition actions from stamp duty.

In the time of McCallum the Criminal Procedure Code was amended. The jurisdiction of the District Court was again extended, allowing it to try certain offences hitherto tried by the Supreme Court.

Owing to complaints regarding the working of the Buddhist Temporalities Ordinance of 1889 Government made inquiries in 1900, and in 1902 proposed certain amendments to improve the administration of Buddhist properties. But Buddhist leaders did not think that such changes would lead to any improvement so long as Government abstained from interference, and the new bill was abandoned. At last in 1904 the Secretary of State waived his objection to Government supervision of the administration of Buddhist properties; and the bill abandoned earlier was adopted with an additional clause empowering the Governor to appoint the Government Agent or the Assistant Government Agent of the district to act as Commissioner for the purpose of assisting the District Committee. This step did not solve the problem completely, and before long Government had to take other steps for the protection of dēvalā and vihārā properties.

Reference has been made to the constitution of Local Boards of Health and Improvement in 1876. The policy of Government at this time was to associate the Government Agent with all the activities of his province for purposes of efficiency, just as in India the Collector was associated with all the activities of his district. The constitution of these Local Boards of Health was vague, and according to it the Government Agent was not bound to be a member. In 1891 the defect was remedied by making the Government Agent an *ex-officio* member and chairman of the Board.

In 1892 small towns which required sanitary measures were given a modified form of local government. The sanitation of these towns was placed under a Sanitary Board, one for each revenue district, the members of these Boards being nominated by the Governor. In 1898 the larger towns were entrusted to Local Boards with greater administrative powers. They consisted of an equal number of elected and nominated members.

The sanitation of towns was improved further during this period. Reference has been made to the supply of water to Colombo from Labugama. At this time a number of other towns such as Kandy, Galle, Nāvalapitiya, Badulla, Ratnapura and Mātalē were provided with pure water supplied from reservoirs. In order to improve further the sanitation of Colombo, a beginning was made in 1903 to provide it with a complete system of drainage and sewage disposal.

Colombo was also provided with other amenities. About 1880 Edison had invented the incandescent lamp which made the electric lighting of houses possible, and had improved the dynamo sufficiently to generate electricity. By 1888 electricity was used in England for lighting houses and streets, and in 1896 there were thirty six companies at work. Two years later electric lighting was introduced in Colombo. Electricity was not used in England immediately for traction. Electric tramways were started in England only about 1895. They were established in Colombo in 1899.

In this manner Government as in previous periods carried on activities which were dictated by humanitarian motives. It aided the social and economic advance of the country by reforming the legal system. It helped the development of agriculture by constructing roads and railways and restoring irrigation works. During this period it took in addition more positive action to improve the state of the country. It raised considerably its own standard of efficiency by reorganizing and expanding its system of administration. It developed the resources of the country by more direct action and raised the physical and intellectual standard of the people by a wide extension of nation-building services.

2. PLANTATIONS, TRADE AND LABOUR

Coffee and cinchona continued to decline during this period, but there was a great expansion in the cultivation of tea, coconuts and rubber.

There was some improvement in cinnamon and cocoa. In the tim of Ridgeway the exports of cinnamon increased by 90 per cent. Those of cocoa went up from 31,000 cwt. in 1896 to 60,000 cwt. in 1902, and the area covered from 21,000 acres to 35,000 acres.

The exports of tobacco increased during the nineties, but external causes led to a decrease early in this century. Tobacco was grown mainly in the Jaffna Peninsula and it was the chief article of trade in the district. It was produced mainly for export and its chief market was Travancore, the people of which preferred the Jaffna product to all others. In 1910 the Travancore Government imposed a heavy protective duty on Ceylon tobacco which nearly ruined it. Later it removed the levy and allowed the import of a certain quota.

The greatest development at this time was in tea, which was helped considerably by the further opening of roads, the extension of the Main Line of the railway to Ūva, and the construction of the Uda Pussällāva and the Kälani Valley Lines. The area under cultivation rose in 1896 to 330,000 acres, in 1900 to 392,000 acres (including Ceylonese gardens), and in 1903 to 406,000 acres. In 1896 the exports of tea amounted to 110,095,000 lb. valued at Rs 51,337,388, which was two-thirds of the total exports. In 1900 they rose to 149,265,053 lb. valued at £3,582,361; and in 1902 to 150,829,000 lb. valued at Rs. 54,298,694 or 56 per cent. of the exports.

Conditions affecting tea deteriorated soon after this. Till 1896 the market of the United Kingdom had continued to expand and had kept pace with the output in India and Ceylon. After that the supply exceeded the demand and the average London price of 8*d*. per lb. in 1896 fell in 1900 to 7*d*., which yielded little profit to the planters. Hence plantations which proved unprofitable owing to their poor yield were abandoned and the planting of new areas was given up.

The situation improved again shortly after. The planters brought down the cost of production by improving the methods of cultivation and manufacture, and by running the plantations on more scientific, efficient and economical lines. New markets were found in the British Dominions, Russia, and China. Exports which had gone down to 149,200,000 lb. in 1903 rose in 1911 to 186,000,000 lb.

There was also a great expansion in the coconut industry mainly in the North-Western, the Western and the Southern Provinces in the Jaffna Peninsula, and along the coast of the Eastern Province. Coconuts were also grown in the Sabaragamuva Province until the planting of rubber spread there. The construction of roads such as the one on the eastern coast, and the extension of the Coast Line railway on the one side to Mātara and on the other to Negombo. and of the Northern Line, assisted the development of the industry very greatly.[1]

The cultivation of rubber had been attempted very early by the Department of the Royal Botanic Gardens, but had not met with much success. In 1876 this Department had obtained a few plants which had grown out of two types of Brazilian rubber seeds planted in the hot houses of Kew Gardens in England, and planted them at Pērādeniya and Heneratgoda. The Ceara rubber plants had flowered first and 977 acres were covered with rubber by 1883 But the plantations did not pay, as the price in London was low and the planters in Ceylon had no experience of rubber cultivation. As a result many of the trees had been replaced by tea; and when the Hevea trees had begun to flower in 1881, their seeds had been sent to other countries. In 1896 the cultivation of Hevea rubber was attempted, and by 1898 the acreage planted covered 1,071 acres. The progress of cultivation was slow as tea flourished at this time and the prospects of rubber were still doubtful.

The situation changed by the end of the century. The experiments conducted by the Royal Botanic Gardens during the year

1. From 1892 exports of the produce of the coconut palm began to increase rapidly. In 1896 exports of coconut-oil, copra, desiccated coconuts, coconuts, poonac and fibre rose to Rs. 11,178,000. In 1911 they went up to Rs. 38,000,000. In 1896 exports of copra amounted to 57,500 cwt. valued at Rs. 550,000. In 1911 they rose to 821,000 cwt. In 1870 coconuts had amounted to 4 per cent. of the total export trade, in 1880 to 9 per cent. and in 1890 to 15 per cent. In 1900 it rose to 17 per cent. and in 1910 to 24·5 per cent.

1899 showed the correct methods of cultivation and manufacture. At the same time the price of tea fell, while that of rubber rose from 2*s.* to 4*s.* per lb. in 1910. During the years 1904 to 1906 it rose further to 6*s.* on account of the development of the rubber industry especially in the United States of America. The cultivation of rubber quickly expanded. In 1900 there were 2,000 acres under cultivation. In 1903 the acreage rose to about 11,600. Of these 10,500 were in the Sabaragamuva Province, which the Kälani Valley railway reached. The remaining 1,100 were in the Western Province. In 1906 the cultivated acreage rose to 50,472, in 1907 to 150,000, and in 1910 to 200,000. Exports of rubber in 1903 amounted to 389 cwt. valued at Rs. 84,784 or Rs. 257·70 per cwt. In 1911 they rose to 61,212 cwt. valued at Rs. 28,000,000. Profits from rubber were very high until about 1907 when the London price fell to 4*s.* per lb. This led to a temporary check in cultivation. The industry expanded again in 1910 when the Brazilian planters forced the price up temporarily to 12*s.* The rubber plantations were opened mainly by European companies, but the Ceylonese took to its cultivation more than to that of tea. Even the poorer classes began to plant their gardens with rubber, sometimes replacing paddy and cinnamon with it.

Trade at this time was not limited to agricultural products. There was the sale of gems. The plumbago industry too expanded during this period. In 1896 the exports amounted to 361,000 tons and rose in 1907 to 538,973 tons.

Government continued to take an interest in the supply of labour because the prosperity of the plantations depended on it and that of Ceylon on the plantations. Government helped to cheapen the cost of labour. It exempted labourers from the road and the gansabhāva taxes, and charged them less than half the normal railway fare. It spent on medical aid a considerable sum of money far exceeding the contribution of the estates. In the time of Ridgeway it provided quarantine camps for labourers who came from India, so that they might not spread infectious diseases in the estates and in the towns through which they passed. In Blake's time it began to contribute Rs. 11,000 per annum towards the expenses of the Labour Commission in India appointed by the Planters' Association to watch the interests of the Ceylon estates.

The main factor against which Government contended at this time was the toll taken by cholera and small-pox. During the years 1889 to 1895 4,634 persons died of cholera and 5,353 of small-pox. The labourers who came by the cheapest and the oldest route, from Pāmban to Mannār by steamer and then by road to Mātalē, if they were infected, generally suffered from diseases on the way and were left behind in the halting-places which were provided for them. Those who pressed on were generally free from infection by the time they reached their destination, and the other labourers in the estates were in no danger of catching the disease from them. However the villagers who lived along the route did suffer, and about 500 of them died of cholera in the district of Mannār alone during the years 1891-1898. In 1897 there was an outbreak of virulent plague in Bombay, and this route was closed in 1900 to prevent the spread of plague in Ceylon.

The real danger to the estates, however, came from labourers who took the sea-route from Tondi, Ammapatam, or Tuticorin in the south coast to Colombo. This route had become increasingly popular, and 80 per cent. of the labourers took it in 1898, the year after a regular steamship service was established between Tuticorin and Colombo. Those who took this route proceeded immediately to the estates by train, at first from Colombo and then from Kälaniya. To prevent the spreading of cholera and small-pox in Colombo and the estates, a quarantine camp was established at Rāgama in 1897. As cases of cholera were common in Tuticorin, a camp was established about the same time nine miles away at Tatparai. Here labourers were medically examined and sent by train to Tuticorin, so that they might embark for Ceylon without being infected at the port. These steps reduced deaths from cholera to 1,207 during the years 1896 to 1902. These camps were maintained till the old route was revived with the construction of the Indo-Ceylon railway, and a quarantine camp was built at Mandapam in South India.

3. IRRIGATION WORKS

The importance of irrigation works was not forgotten with the departure of Gordon. Havelock realized the necessity for their restoration to develop the neglected regions of the island and to preserve the life and health of those who lived there. Ridgeway was no less concerned with the welfare of the peasants. Taking advantage of the increasing revenue and the extension of the railway to the north, he carried out schemes with even greater zeal than his predecessors. The works begun by him, when completed, made over 162,000 acres irrigable and the production of 3,240,000 bushels of paddy possible in one crop. Blake too was interested in irrigation, but he made an important change in Government's policy. He found that many of the existing schemes had insufficient catchment areas and distributing channels. He decided to complete and develop these schemes before starting new ones. McCallum extended irrigation, which hitherto served paddy cultivation, to the plantation of products like coconuts.

In the Northern Province major irrigation works first received attention in the time of Ridgeway. The chief restoration in the area was that of the Giant's Tank. It covered 4,425 acres and its bund was 9½ miles long. Its storage capacity amounted to 1,046,000,000 cubic feet, and it was capable of irrigating 20,000 acres. The channels connected with this tank were opened in the time of Blake, and they made 22,965 more acres irrigable. Other schemes begun by Ridgeway were the Kanukkeni works, south of Mullaitīvu, and the Karachchi scheme which was capable of irrigating 20,000 acres.

The Karachchi works were mainly the result of the extension of the railway to the north. The same cause also led to the extension of irrigation in the North-Central Province. The Nāchchadūva Tank, fed by the Malvatu Oya, was restored by Ridgeway to irrigate 20,000 acres. This scheme was continued by Blake who repaired the Nuvaraväva, also fed by the same river, to irrigate 63,000 acres. To complete this scheme the Mahagalkadavala Tank, fed by the Kandarā Oya, the tributary of the Malvatu Oya, and the surplus water of the Nuvaraväva, was restored. Another important tank restored by Ridgeway was the Minnēriya in the Tamankaduva District capable of irrigating 15,000 acres. A very large number of village tanks too were repaired both in the North-Central and the North-Western Provinces.

Three large irrigation schemes were carried out in the North-Western, the Ūva and the Central Provinces. Havelock began the Däduru Oya project, which was extended by Blake to irrigate another 3,770 acres, Havelock was also responsible for the restoration of the Madurukätiya channel of the Kumbukkan Oya near Buttala in Ūva. The Minipē Äla scheme in the Central Province to irrigate 2,000 acres was begun by McCallum.

Irrigation works were carried out on a much larger scale in the Eastern Province, where roads were constructed along the coast north and south of Batticaloa. In the time of Ridgeway the Kantalai and the Rukam (west of Batticaloa) schemes were continued, and the Sakamam (west of Tirukkovil) scheme was undertaken. The construction of two entirely new tanks, the Vakanēri (west of Kalkudah) to irrigate 13,000 acres, and the Unichchai to irrigate 19,000 acres, was also begun in his time and completed in the time of Blake. Blake carried out also the Kondavattavan Scheme, connected with the Pattipolai-āru, west of the Amparai Tank, to irrigate 12,600 acres, while McCallum commenced the Allai Scheme south of Kottiyar Bay to irrigate 3,250 acres. The extent of land irrigable in the Eastern Province at the beginning of Ridgeway's rule was 68,000 acres. He increased it by 48,000 acres and sold 20,000 acres of paddy land.

The Southern Province too received considerable attention. The works connected with the Tissamaharâma Tank, the restoration of which had originally been planned by Ward, were extended further by Ridgeway, increasing the area irrigable to 7,000 acres. Another important scheme extended at this time was that connected with the Valavē Ganga, stretching from Uggalkaltota in the Sabaragamuva Province almost to the mouth of the river. These works referred to earlier were begun in 1886 and continued in the time of Havelock. Under Ridgeway the scheme was extended further, making the total area irrigable over 10,000 acres. Blake extended the Kirindi Oya scheme by constructing a channel on the right bank to irrigate 12,500 acres.

Another important event which falls within this period is the abolition of the grain tax. This tax had been the main source of revenue of the Anurādhapura and Polonnaruva kings. Before the British occupation it was paid in kind, and the amount depended on the crop. As it was now fixed and was paid in cash, many thousands during bad seasons did not pay the tax, or fell into the hands of money-lenders in their attempts to pay it. The result was that the lands of these persons went back to Government for non-payment of tax, or to money-lenders whom they could not repay. The tax had been opposed for some time by George Wall, and its abolition in 1893 proved beneficial to the peasants.

4. TRANSPORT AND COMMUNICATIONS

The increase in plantations, the growth of trade, the expansion of the activities of Government and the general prosperity of the country led to a great development in communications in all parts

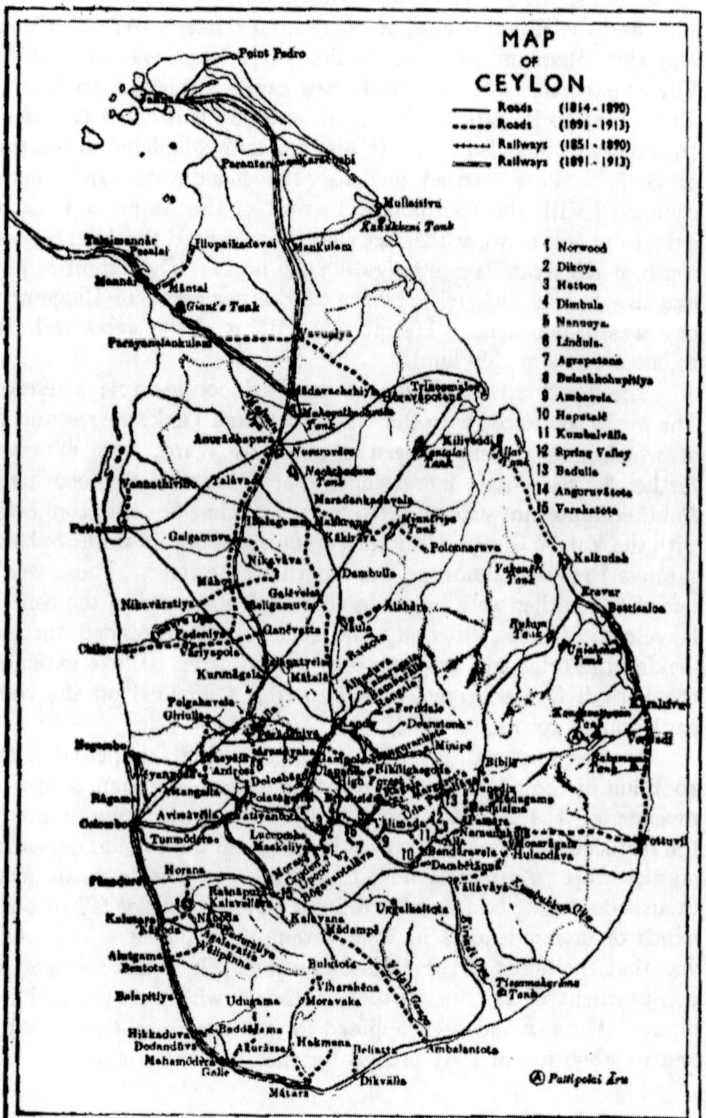
MAP
OF
CEYLON
Roads (1814-1890)
Roads (1891-1913)
Railways (1851-1890)
Railways (1891-1913)
1 Norwood
2 Dikoya
3 Hatton
4 Dimbula
5 Nanuoya.
6 Lindula.
7 Agrapatana
8 Bulathkohupitiya
9 Ambavela.
10 Haputalē
11 Kumbalvālla
12 Spring Valley
13 Badulla
14 Anguruvātota
15 Varakatota
Point Pedro
Paranthan
Mullaitivu
Talaimannār
Pesalai
Illupaikadavai
Mankulam
Mannār
Māntai
Giant's Tank
Vavuniya
Parayanalankulam
Trincomalee
Anurādhapura
Nuvaravāva
Nachchaduwa Tank
Kiliveddi
Vannathivillu
Talāvā
Maradankadavala
Puttalam
Galgamuva
Kekirāva
Polonnaruva
Kalkudah
Nikavāva
Dambulla
Eravur
Batticaloa
Nikavāratiya
Galēvela
Naula
Chilaw
Rattota
Kurunāgala
Mātalē
Polgahavela
Giriulla
Kandy
Negombo
Bibile
Rāgama
Colombo
Avissāvēla
Tunmōdera
Lucombe
Maskeliya
Passara
Pottuvil
Horana
Pānadura
Kalutara
Ratnapura
Kalavāna
Mādampē
Aluthgama
Bentota
Balapitiya
Bulutota
Uduguma
Moravaka
Hikkaduva
Dodandūva
Baddēgama
Akurāssa
Hakmana
Beliatta
Ambalantota
Mahamōdera
Galle
Mātara
Dikvālla
Pattipolai Āru

of the island. They were built partly to help the expansion of the cultivation of tea, rubber and coconut, and partly to develop the other parts of the country in which Government was becoming increasingly interested. In fact at this time all other developments depended on them.

Road construction made great headway during this period. In the Central Province roads were built in 1903 from Dimbula to Lindula and from Lindula to Agrapatana, to open for tea the south-eastern part of the Nuvara Eliya District. The road from Nuvara Eliya to St. Margaret's in the eastern part of the same district was extended to Uda Pussällāva, and in 1903 a branch road was built from Brookside northwards to High Forest. The area around Adam's Peak was developed still further. A road from Norwood southwards to Upcot was begun in 1893 and completed in 1898. About the same time roads were built from Maskeliya north-west to Luccombe, south-east to Cruden, and southwards to Moray. In 1908 Dolosbāgē was made accessible by another road from Gampola. In the Mātalē District the Teldeniya-Rangala road was extended in 1895 to Ferndale. Another road in the same district completed about the same time was from Nāula on the Mātalē-Dambulla road to Ālahära. But this was constructed not to help the plantations but to open up the region for paddy cultivation. In order to improve communications further, three important bridges were built over the Mahaväli Ganga near Ulapanē at Pērādeniya, and at Bōvagamuva below Kandy. The one at Pērādeniya replaced the historic satinwood bridge built in 1832.

In the Western Province in the Kalutara District where land was being opened for coconuts and rubber, the road from Horana to Alutgama by way of Anguruvātota was completed. The Matugama-Agalavatta road was extended to Badureliya and further to Atval Oya in 1896, and from Agalavatta northwards to Kalavellāva ferry in 1912. In 1906 Nāgoda was connected with Nāboda. Two other roads were built in the northern part of the Western Province. Attanagalla was connected with Veyangoda in 1891 and with Pasyāla in 1900, thus connecting both these towns with Ruanvälla. In 1891 the bridge over the Attanagalu Oya was completed; in 1894 the Victoria Bridge was built over the Kälani Ganga giving another means of access to Colombo; the third bridge was at Tunmōdera near Labugama.

In the Sabaragamuva Province in 1897 Kāgalla was connected with Bulathkohupitiya to help the plumbago industry in the latter place. The prospect of the extension of the railway to Yatiyantota led to the improvement of the road from Yatiyantota to Polatagama, and its extension to Ardross to enable traffic from Western Dolosbāgē to reach Yatiyantota. The important bridges built in this province were over the Ritigaha Oya (1898), and at Varakatota near Ratnapura. In the Ratnapura District a road was built from Mādampē along the Valavē Ganga as far as Ambalantota in the Southern Province. This road was completed in 1905 and helped the development of irrigation works along the river. In the Southern Province no other important roads were built; but large bridges were constructed at Bentota in 1903, at Mahamōdera near Galle in 1902, and near Mātara in 1906.

In the Province of Ūva in 1894 a road was built from Nāula on the Bandāravela-Badulla road eastwards to Spring Valley. In the same year Kumbalvälla on the same road was connected with Namunukula through Älla. This road was extended in 1898 to Passara, which in 1893 had been connected with Madulsīma. In 1899 this road was extended to Dunedin. In 1906 a road was built from Haputalē eastwards to Dambētänna, another tea area. The extension of the railway to Ūva led to the construction of two roads. The Nuvara Eliya-Välimada road was connected with Ambēvela, and in 1912 Bandāravela with Välimada. Eastern Ūva also received attention. The Vällavāya-Moneragala road was gravelled and extended to Pottuvil in the Eastern Province. In 1907 Bibilē was connected with this road again by extending this road from Bibilē to Mädagama as far as Hulandāva. In the Eastern Province only one other important road was built. It was built along the coast north and south of Batticaloa, enabling the development of irrigation and of coconut plantations. The north road was built up to Kiliveddi ferry in 1903 and the south road was extended to the Nāval-ār in 1905.

In the North-Western Province, Vāriyapola on the Kandy-Puttalam road was connected in 1905 with the railway station at Ganēvatta and later with Chilaw. In 1906 Nikaväratiya was connected with Māho. A road was built also on the west coast from Puttalam to Vannathivillu. To help traffic further a bridge was built in 1902 at Dandagamuva In the North-Central Province two important roads were completed in 1900. Ihalagama on the Talāva-Kākirāva road was connected with Galēvela, which was already joined to the Mātalē-Dambulla road at Palāpatvela. The other road, from Habarana to Polonnaruva, was begun in 1891. For the first road a large bridge was built at Beligamuva near Galēvela.

In the Northern Province, Vavuniya was connected with Parayanalan-kulam on the Mānnär-Mädavachchiya road. Along the coast a road was built in 1901 from Māntai to Illuppaikadavai. In 1905 Parantan was linked with Karachchi where irrigation was being developed. In 1906 the Mädavachchiya-Mānnar road was extended to Pesalai.

Considerable attention was also paid during this period to the improvement of country roads. In 1890 there were 1,635 miles of metalled road, 965 miles of graveı ed road, and 542 miles of forest clearings or natural road making a total of 3,142 miles. In 1912 there were 2,772 miles of metalled road, 277 miles of track-metalled road, 515 miles of gravelled road and 319 miles of natural road, making a total of 3,883 miles. The metalling of the North Road was completed in 1891 and of the Kandy-Trincomalee road in 1898. The Anurādhapura-Trincomalee road was metalled in 1905 to suit motor traffic. In the time of Ridgeway the Central, North-Central, Ūva and Sabaragamuva Provinces received most attention. About 300 new bridges were built and about 400 timber bridges were converted into permanent structures In Blake's time the Western, North-Central, and Eastern Provinces received most attention. In these 43, 42 and 24 miles respectively were converted into metalled roads. The number of iron bridges built in his time was 427. In the time of McCallum 36 new roads were taken in hand and 22 were completed. The number of bridges built was about 500.

In the earlier periods roads had been used mainly by pedestrians, bullock carts and horse coaches. In 1896 they began to be used by cyclists, and in the time of McCallum by motor vehicles. From 1816 a primitive form of the bicycle had been used in England. About 1865 this had been replaced by the 'tall ordinary' or 'penny farthing', a few of which were introduced into Ceylon. The modern type of bicycle was invented in 1876, but it became popular only about 1890 when the pneumatic tyre was adopted. A few years later this type came into use in Ceylon.

The first road automobile was built as far back as 1769. Steam coaches were tried about the same time as railways, but did not become popular owing to various difficulties. In the seventies kerosene oil came into use. In preparing this for oil-engines, a crude petroleum benzine or petrol was also produced. Using this volatile spirit Daimler produced a high-speed engine, and used it for a motor-bicycle in 1886 and for a motor car in 1887. The motor vehicle however did not become popular in England till the end of the nineteenth century. Early in the twentieth century it began to be used in Ceylon. Some estates replaced the bullock cart by motor lorries. The Postal Department used motor cars to convey mails between Anurādhapura and Trincomalee, and Government officials began to use them for their travelling.

The introduction of motor vehicles demanded further improvements in roads. The metalled surface had to be widened, sharp bends had to be avoided, and in hilly parts the gradient had to be regulated. The toll-stations which had come into existence with the expansion of roads were abolished in 1910 as they delayed traffic at regular intervals.

The construction of railways went hand in hand with roads. The Sea Coast Line had been continued to Bentota in 1890. It was extended to Alutgama in 1891, to Galle in 1894, and to Mātāra in 1895, thus connecting the important coastal towns in the Western and the Southern Provinces. The Main Line was extended to Haputalē in 1893 and to Bandāravela in 1899. Thus Ūva was connected with Colombo, and its products were provided with a quicker and cheaper means of transport.

Five new lines were built during this period. A line to the north was built from Polgahavela. It reached Kurunāgala in 1894, Anurādhapura in 1900, and Jaffna in 1905. This line linked Colombo with the chief towns of the North-Western, the North-Central and the Northern Provinces. It helped the opening of some of the areas of jungle land which it traversed and the cultivation of coconut and paddy in them. It connected the thickly populated districts of the north with the rest of the island, breaking up the isolation of Jaffna and helping to relieve its congestion. Above all it enabled the Tamils of the north to realize more fully their connection with the rest of the people in Ceylon.

In 1913 a branch line was constructed from Mädavachchiya to Talaimannār. This ensured a safer means of communication between India and Ceylon in time of war. It quickened the growth of trade with India, and enabled Colombo to be used as a port for South India. It facilitated the immigration of Indian labourers who once more took to this route, gradually abandoning the voyage from Tuticorin to Colombo.

The Kälani Valley Line was built to help the rubber, tea and coconut plantations. It was begun in 1900, opened as far as Avissāvēlla in 1902, and extended to Yatiyantota in 1903. The extension from Avissāvēlla to Ratnapura was made in 1912. To reduce expenditure in construction, the narrow gauge of 2 feet 6 inches was adopted on this line. The nature of the country required 57 bridges for the first part of the line up to Yatiyantota. Another narrow gauge line was built from Nānuoya to Rāgala to feed the tea district of Uda Pussällāva. It was begun in 1903 and completed in 1906.

A railway was built from Rāgama to Negombo, to be extended to Puttalam, to serve the areas planted with coconut which it traversed. It was begun in 1907, opened up to Jāäla in 1908, and extended to Negombo in 1909.

Railway expansion during this period was mainly in Ridgeway's time when the capital invested in new railways amounted to Rs. 7,745,104. A part of the cost of the Kälani Valley and the Uda Pussällāva lines was met by a loan received in 1902. In 1896 there were 297 miles of railway. By 1903 the number of miles rose to 386, and by 1905 to 562. The Northern Line alone meant an addition of 160 miles. These lines led to the construction of a large number of approach roads. For instance in 1904 a sum of Rs. 361,781 was spent on them.

From the beginning the railway was a paying concern. Its receipts went up in 1891 and continued to rise both on account of goods and passenger traffic. In 1894 they rose to Rs. 5,572,054, and in 1903 to about Rs. 8,000,000 or 28 per cent. more than in 1895. The profit from 1862 to 1902 amounted to Rs. 33,000,000.

Telegraph communication too was extended between 1890 and 1913. In Havelock's time lines were constructed to Maskeliya, Bōgavantalāva, and Agrapatana. In the time of Ridgeway another 500 miles of line were laid. The line to Puttalam was extended to Mannār; and that to Anurādhapura through Vavuniya to Jaffna, and from there to Point Pedro and Kankēsanturai. The line to Ratnapura was extended to Haputalē. Colombo was linked with Nuvara Eliya by a line through Ramboda, and a duplicate line was constructed from Colombo to Kalutara. In 1895 there were 59 telegraph offices. In the time of Ridgeway, their number rose to 88. Before Blake left Ceylon, 16 more offices were established. In the time of McCallum about 50 railway telegraph offices were opened to the public. During Ridgeway's period the number of telegrams increased by 168 per cent. This was partly due to the reduction of the rate for local telegrams from 40 cents to 25 cents in 1897, and of that to England from 4*s*. to 2*s*. 6*d*. in 1902.

Telephone communication was established about this time. In 1892 the Postal Department took over the telegraph lines in Ceylon, which hitherto were under the control of the Government of India. In 1896 it took over also the plant of the Oriental Telephone Company. The telephone had been invented by Graham Bell in 1876 and the first telephone exchange in England had been set up in 1879. But the use of the telephone did not spread rapidly as its value depended on the number of persons who installed the instrument. During the time of Blake all public offices in Colombo were connected with telephones. In the time of McCallum the lines in Colombo were placed underground, and trunk lines were constructed to Kandy and Nuvara Eliya, and extended to Galaha, Kalutara and Galle. Exchanges were established at Kandy, Nuvara Eliya, Anurādhapura, Galle and Kalutara.

In the time of McCallum a wireless station was established in Colombo with a range of 450 miles. The first wireless message was transmitted by Marconi in 1897 and signals were sent across the Atlantic in 1901. Thus it did not take many years for Ceylon to benefit by this new invention.

The Colombo Harbour was improved further during this time. As far back as 1878 even before the south-west breakwater was completed, it was realized that the area sheltered would soon prove insufficient. Reference has been made to the increase of shipping from 1883 In 1893 as provision for further anchorage became an urgent necessity, the construction of a north-east breakwater of 1,000 feet and a north-west breakwater of 2,670 feet was sanctioned. The work was begun in March 1896. Ten years later both breakwaters were completed, and the area of shelter was increased from 415 acres to 660 acres.

The shelter of the northern area enabled the construction of a graving dock of 700 feet for cleaning and repairing ships. Begun in 1899, it was completed in 1906. It cost £408,022, towards which the Admiralty contributed £159,000. As a result of these improvements Colombo became the largest and the finest port in Asia.

The number of ships which entered Colombo Harbour increased further during this period. It rose from 2,144 in 1896 to 2,254 in 1911. In 1891 the tonnage was 5,696,948. In 1907 it rose to 6,196,116, and in 1911 to 7,036,625. This expansion in trade and other commercial needs of the town led to the reclamation of the section of the Beira Lake between Captain's Garden and Galle Face.

5. EDUCATION

The spread of education continued during this period. In 1912 the number of Government schools rose to 5 English schools, 19 Anglo-Vernacular schools and 778 Vernacular schools, and Grant-in-aid schools to 187 English schools, 31 Anglo-Vernacular schools, and 1,782 Vernacular schools. In all there were 802 Government schools with 84,844 boys and 23,997 girls, and 2,000 Grant-in-aid schools with 152,993 boys and 77,365 girls. Thus there were 339,199 pupils besides 35,402 in 1,533 unregistered schools. In the same year 202,885 scholars attended Vernacular schools, 7,853 Anglo-Vernacular schools, and 26,099 English schools.[1] In 1891 the percentage of literacy was 19·9, in 1901 it was 21·7, and in 1911 it was 26·4.

At first the expansion was not rapid. From 1892 to 1902 Government schools had increased only by 13·7 per cent. and Grant-in-aid schools by 39 per cent., though the rate of grants, which had been reduced annually till 1895, had once more been raised. Therefore in 1904 Government appointed a Commission to put forward proposals for the spread of vernacular education. The Commission examined the subject from the point of view of finance and local organization, and the proposals it made were carried out with a few modifications by the Rural and Town Schools Ordinances of 1907. It also made some recommendations regarding other questions like the medium of instruction, the lack of qualified teachers, and the

1 In 1869 there were only 26 girls' schools, and in 1870 there were only 385 Government and Grant-in-aid schools and 16,927 pupils.

relation of education imparted in schools to the opportunities open to pupils after they leave school, but these led to no important results.

The main proposals of the Commission were that vernacular education should be provided for the male population as a whole. and where schools existed attendance should be made compulsory in aided as well as in Government schools. As Government could not compel children to attend schools where instruction in religions other than their own was imparted, the Commission recommended that religious instruction should be withheld from pupils belonging to denominations other than that of the schools they attended. To prevent the neglect of education in any area, it recommended that the opening of schools for boys should be made compulsory in every place where the population was sufficiently large. The Commission did not ignore the education of girls. It recommended that education should gradually be made compulsory for them, beginning with the Western, the Southern and the North-Western Provinces.

The Ordinances of 1907 was enforced in all districts except Jaffna and Mullaitīvu. School Committees with Government Agents as chairmen were established to draw up schemes for the establishment of vernacular schools, and to make bye-laws to enforce compulsory attendance. Vernacular education was thereafter steadily extended to rural districts and attendance in schools was improved. During the years 1908 to 1912 Government established 189 schools, and the number of pupils rose by nearly 50 per cent.

There was also a rapid increase in the number of English schools. The revival of Buddhism and Hinduism went on. The Buddhists continued to publish journals in Sinhalese and carry on controversies with Christians, as well as among themselves, with regard to the propriety of their own religious customs and practices such as the worship of gods. The Hindus too continued their activities, and before the end of this period the *Hindu Organ* became a bi-weekly and its Tamil edition a weekly paper. Under these circumstances one would have expected a further advance in vernacular education, but both Buddhists and Hindus took to English education as much as the Christians.

The reason is not far to seek. Though Government and the Missions took pains to spread vernacular education, they made no serious attempt to change the curriculum of vernacular schools to suit the changes that were taking place in the country. Further a knowledge of Sinhalese or Tamil did not take students very far. Classical Sinhalese literary works were written in a language no longer spoken, and their subject-matter did not differ much from that of medieval European literature. Usually Sinhalese works, unless they were translations of European works, did not deal with modern topics or subjects discussed in newspapers. Tamil literature was more progressive, but did not satisfy modern needs much more than Sinhalese. Besides as the small minority who took to higher education began to confine themselves during this period to English and Western studies, the vernaculars instead of being improved began to be neglected. On the other hand the opening of the Suez Canal, the establishment of the submarine cable and the development of communications increased contact with the West, a knowledge of which was available in Ceylon only through the medium of English, English was also the language of Government, the law courts, trade and commerce, and no man without knowing English could follow with interest the developments in the country. Finally at this time an education in English opened vast avenues for employment. The work in the courts was quickly increasing. Hospitals and dispensaries were growing in number. Plantations were being opened, and trade and commerce were being developed. Government services were expanding in an unprecedented manner. All these demanded men with a knowledge of English, and the growing middle class pursued an English education to take advantage of these opportunities.

The connection of education in English schools with England was strengthened further during this period. Even after the Cambridge examinations were introduced into Ceylon, schools in the north continued to prepare pupils for the Calcutta and Madras examinations. In 1907 as a result of the Curzon Commission on Education, colleges were assigned to universities according to territory, and those in Ceylon were placed under Madras. In the meantime the railway had been opened to Jaffna and the colleges in the north began to fall into line with those in the rest of the island. In 1906 some of them began to prepare for the Cambridge examinations, and in 1911 Jaffna College which taught up to the degree standard severed its connection with the Madras University.

Further changes were made regarding government scholarships. In 1895 it was decided to award them on the results of an examination conducted by an Oxford and Cambridge Joint Board.

In 1906 this too was abandoned and two annual scholarships were awarded on the results of the London Intermediate Examinations. In 1880 the Colombo Academy had begun to teach science, and in 1905 chemistry and physics laboratories had been established in the Technical College. To promote the study of science one of these scholarships was awarded to science students.

Steps were taken to improve the teaching in English schools. At this time there were no trained teachers or graduates, as in India, to man the schools. In 1903 Government established a College for the training of teachers. In 1911 it appointed a commit tee and got down an expert from England to report on English schools. They proposed far reaching changes in the methods of instruction and examination. To make education more effective, they recommended better provision for higher education by the establishment of a University College.

English schools suffered also from other defects. The establishment, often in the same town, of a number of denominational schools led to much competition. Schools did not concentrate on the needs of the pupils as a whole but on those who had a chance of rising to the top of the educational ladder. One of the inspectors remarked that on examining schools in 1903 he was impressed with the notion that most of them were employed in performing a routine march to Oxford and Cambridge Universities, which more than 99·8 per cent. of the children had no prospect of reaching. Hence many useful subjects like commerce were neglected. This spirit of competition entered even the girls' schools. They did not promote an education suitable for girls, but each school tried to compete with the others in the number of candidates presented at the Cambridge examinations.

In emphasizing the Cambridge examinations, English schools in the Sinhalese districts followed a curriculum more suited to England than to Ceylon. They devoted attention to Western classical and modern European languages rather than to Sinhalese. At the end of this period an attempt was made to encourage the study of Sinhalese by means of grants, but it did not lead to any important result. Schools in Jaffna did not at first take to the Cambridge examinations partly because the connection with Madras enabled them to have a curriculum more suited to their environment. It at least enabled them to develop Tamil studies. But once they adopted the Cambridge examinations, they too had to follow a curriculum more suited to English conditions. In fact from the very beginning the aim of English education had been to equip persons for employment under Government. This utilitarian aim continued to predominate the minds of parents as well as of pupils and teachers.

Thus English schools paid very little attention to the culture of the people. Christian schools, whether English or vernacular, almost ignored it. They did not teach Buddhism or Hinduism. Buddhism was closely interwoven with the culture of the Sinhalese. 'All their stories of home and childhood', wrote R. S. Copleston,[1] 'all their national literature, all that was grand to them in history and science, the conquests of their kings, the great buildings of their country: all were engaged in the interests of Buddhism'. Hinduism was similarly associated with the culture of the Tamils. And the exclusion of Buddhism and Hinduism in Christian schools also meant the disregard of the past heritage of the Sinhalese and the Tamils.

These defects began to be remedied in Buddhist and Hindu schools, whose number grew during this period. In 1907 the Buddhist Theosophical Society conducted 178 schools. The Saiva Paripālana Sabhai also established a number of schools. Buddhist schools taught Buddhism and Hindu schools Hinduism. But the changes they effected did not make a serious difference to the country immediately.

The standard of studies both in the Medical and Law Colleges, which furnished almost all the doctors and lawyers needed in Ceylon, was raised during this period. The Medical College was established in 1870 on the proposal of Dr. Loos, who wanted medical assistance placed within the reach of the people of backward areas. Since then it had supplied doctors and apothecaries for the hospitals and dispensaries. In 1901 its curriculum was revised, and the following year the College was reorganized and provided with new laboratories. The courses at the Law College were improved in 1896, and in 1906 university examinations were substituted for the preliminary examination.

The importance of technical education for India had been emphasized both by the Despatch of the Court of Directors of 1854 as well as by the Commission of 1882, but it had suffered from lack of clear thinking on the part of Government and the public. In

1. R. S. Copleston was Bishop of Colombo and later Metropolitan of India. He is the author of *Buddhism in Magadha and Ceylon*.

Ceylon conditions were not very different. A Technical College was established in 1893. In 1896 it had only ten pupils in civil and mechanical engineering. It did not attract pupils as the courses led to no definite opening or employment. In 1897 it was reorganized to provide a training ground for recruits to the chief government technical departments such as the Public Works, the Survey, the Railway, and the Telegraph, and in 1903 the numbers rose to 254. In 1905 with the addition of chemistry and physics laboratories the preliminary work of medical students was carried out by the College. Agricultural education received even less attention. The School of Agriculture instead of being improved was abolished in 1901 as it failed to attract the sons of landowners.

6. SOCIAL CHANGES AND THE REFORM OF THE LEGISLATIVE COUNCIL

During the nineteenth century British rule did not result in any important change in the condition of the peasants who formed more than ninety per cent. of the indigenous population. Owing to the negative policy of Government the main functions of the grades of Ceylonese officials who ruled in the rural areas did not differ much from those exercised in pre-British times. It was in the interest of these officials to retain the old social system, and many of them did not encourage the spread of education or the dissolution of the caste system. It is true their work was directed and controlled by British Government Agents. But with the expansion of their duties and of their work in offices, these British officers began to rely more and more on their Ceylonese subordinates, and though they made a regular annual tour of their districts they failed to keep in touch sufficiently with the needs of the people.

At the beginning of the twentieth century there was undoubtedly some improvement in the condition of the villagers. Even in the remote districts of the North-Central, the North-Western, the Ūva, the Sabaragamuva and the Eastern Provinces and the Vanni, where few roads existed, the development of irrigation works provided a supply of water for cultivating fields, while the extension of medical facilities helped to improve health. For instance, in 1892 there were only 2 hospitals and 9 dispensaries in the North-Central Province; in 1902 the number of dispensaries was 38. There were only a few schools in these areas, but the villagers were beginning to appreciate them. Not only did they ask for more but also in many places they themselves provided the buildings. But in these areas the ways of life of the peasants changed little.

In the Central Province there were greater signs of change. Many began to replace their thatched cottages with tile-roofed brick houses. Men who belonged to the backward castes ceased to be satisfied with the loin cloth alone as their dress. With the development of roads and railways to meet the needs of the plantations, they began to extend their vision beyond the limits of their village. Owing to their contact with the low-country people in the towns, they developed a commercial spirit. They began to cultivate vegetables for the local market, and plant in their gardens tea, cocoa, cardamoms, and pepper, for sale to traders. During the years 1890 to 1902 they cultivated more than 6,000 acres with cocoa. But few took to actual trade or crafts. There were yet few schools in the area and the people were little affected by Western thought. Caste continued to influence them, and they clung to the view that the dignity of land was paramount and cultivation was the highest form of work.

The Jaffna peninsula continued on the whole to be the land of the Vellāla. Here no plantations of tea or coffee arose to bring about a radical economic change. Buttressed by Hindu beliefs, caste ideas and practices prevailed, and here too the cultivators did not take to trade or crafts. However, new forces succeeded in making a few inroads into the ancient social system. The work of Christian Missions, the levelling influence of education, the rise of labourers' wages, all had their effect. Some persons outside the Vellāla group who were not attached to the land took to new enterprises, and these new rich began to rebel against caste rules and prejudices.

Changes in the Western and the Southern Provinces which resulted from the influences of the West have been noticed in earlier chapters. After 1882 when Galle ceased to be the port for steamers, the Western Province forged ahead, helped by the growth of trade and the expansion of government departments.

The most noteworthy social change of this period is the quick rise of the middle class. Reference has been made to the growth of the legal profession since 1833 and of the medical profession since 1870. With the increase of English schools the number of teachers rapidly increased. The expansion of government departments and the growth of mercantile houses led to the employment of a large number of clerks, and the expansion of agricultural industries to a rise in the number of planters, contractors, transport agents, merchants and traders.

The middle class lived mainly in the towns and formed a fairly large community along the western seaboard and in the Jaffna peninsula. Most of its members had acquired an English education, and owing to their enlightenment and wealth exercised a considerable influence in the country. But they had no share in Government which was spreading its tentacles in all directions and disturbing their life in various ways. Almost all the higher government posts were filled by British officials, who along with the British merchants and planters now formed a superior caste. In the rural areas the administration of the country was confined almost wholly to the descendants of the ancient ruling class, who naturally had little sympathy with the aspirations of people who tried to displace them.

The middle class of course refused to be satisfied with its lot. Conscious of the positive rights it possessed as a result of the equality in law established in 1833, it began to resent the special privileges enjoyed by the British and the members of the ancient ruling families. The victory of Japan against Russia in 1904 showed that Easterners, if properly trained and equipped, could hold their own against Westerners. Sinhalese and Tamils who attended English schools studied English history and the development of parliamentary institutions, and did not see any reason why they should not control the legislature as the British middle class did after the Reform Bill of 1832. The Indian Legislative Councils in which unofficials were included only in 1861, had been reformed in 1892 permitting Indians to elect some of their members on a geographical basis. They had been reformed again in 1909 with an extension of the right of election. At the same time Indians had been included in the Executive Councils both of the Viceroy and of the Governors of the Presidencies. Yet in Ceylon there had been no changes, though the proportion of literacy of those educated in English was much higher than in India. Imbued with Liberal ideas, Colebrooke had not only proposed a reform of the system of administration, but had also recommended at the same time the establishment of a Legislative Council so that the administrators might be responsive to public opinion. Since his time the administrative system had been unified further with the construction of roads and railways. An effective system of provincial government had been established based on differences in geographical and economic conditions. The economic resources of the country had been developed, and by a common system of administration the interests of the people had been welded together as no previous Government had done. In most of these reforms the peoples of Ceylon had been treated as if they were one nation, but Government had made no corresponding change in the Legislative Council

The middle class whose leaders were influenced by British Liberal ideas began to ask for a reform of the Legislative Council. A parliamentary system of government had been demanded and refused earlier on the ground that Government would have then come under the control of the Europeans and the Burghers who formed but a fraction of the population. The agitation now came mainly from the Sinhalese and the Tamils. They did not concern themselves with the military contribution which had been gradually raised from 1891 and had been fixed in 1898 at nine and a half per cent. of the revenue. They did not demand an unofficial majority to control the executive. They requested the abolition of racial representation, and the introduction of a territorial system of representation which would have brought the Legislative Council into line with the changes already made in the administrative system. As a result of British rule the interests of the people differed not so much according to race but geographically, and John Ferguson, an European member of the Legislative Council, had advocated territorial representation as far back as 1887. The Sinhalese and the Tamils also demanded representation by election instead of by nomination, so that the members of the Legislative Council might be truly representative of the people. As recommended by Ridgeway, they asked for the inclusion of unofficials in the Executive Council so that they might have a voice in the inner counsels of Government. They did not ignore the interests of the Europeans. They approved of a member each for the Planters' Association and the Chamber of Commerce, and the reservation of a few seats for minorities like the Burghers and the Muslims.

The Government of Ceylon did not sympathize at all with these moderate demands. The British were not influenced now by Liberal ideas of popular government to the same extent as in the days of Colebrooke. They were influenced by ideas of imperialism, and did not contemplate handing over the government of the colonies in the near future to their inhabitants. Besides colonies were no longer looked upon merely as places held in trust by Government for the welfare of their inhabitants, but also as the most lucrative outlet for the accumulated capital and the manufactured goods of the British people.

The Government of Ceylon, like the Indian Government of the days of Curzon, made almost a cult of efficiency. The Industrial Revolution had led to the adoption of scientific methods in administration, and the competition among the industrial powers had led to an emphasis on efficiency in government in Europe. British officials of this time, who came imbued with these ideas of efficiency and found that the bureaucratic system lent itself to the development of efficient methods of government, thought that the advance Ceylon had made under a bureaucracy was itself an argument against a popular form of government. They no longer considered like Colebrooke that the legislature ought to keep pace with administrative development. On the contrary they did not want the efficiency of Government lowered in any way by the interference of amateurs.

There was a third reason why the British did not view with favour the demands made by the middle class. The evil effects of the Industrial Revolution had led them gradually to take a greater interest in the welfare of the working classes, and in 1867 they had enfranchised their urban workers and in 1884 their rural workers. Hence they were not willing to give a considerable voice in the government of Ceylon to a small middle class, who to some extent had cut themselves away from the rest of the population.

In short the Government of Ceylon did not take a long view of the matter. It did not think that it was its duty gradually to prepare the people of Ceylon to take over the government as the earlier Liberals did. It did not consider that there was any need for changes of a constitutional character, to follow up and complete the work begun by their administrative changes in the matter of welding the peoples of Ceylon into one nation. On the other hand it considered that any reform should be with the object of improving the efficiency of the administration. People were divided into communities between which there was little or no intermarriage. The larger communities had representatives in the Legislative Council, and Government had allowed itself to be influenced by their views and given them considerable satisfaction. The new educated Ceylonese middle class was unrepresented in the Council, and Government thought all that was necessary was to associate this new community with Government by giving it a representative. It also recommended the addition of another member for the Low-country Sinhalese, whose numbers and importance had grown. It did not approve of election either. Already the European members were nominated from those chosen by European associations. If the Burghers and the educated Ceylonese too organized themselves similarly, they could select their members and submit their names to Government.

The Secretary of State agreed on the whole with the recommendations made by McCallum. But he probably did not wish to refuse altogether to Ceylon what had been granted to India. He allowed the right of election to the Europeans, the Burghers and the educated Ceylonese. He refused to continue the third European seat. In the meantime the Ceylon Tamils considered the probable results of the proposals of Government and pointed out that with a population of over 9½ lakhs the Tamils would have only one representative, while the Sinhalese with a little over 23 lakhs would have four members as the Educated Ceylonese seat too would go to them. On McCallum's recommendation the Tamils too were given an additional member.

The reformed Council came into existence in 1912. The only new features were the introduction of the elective principle and the enfranchisement of the Sinhalese and Tamil middle class. The Burghers had always been a middle-class body. The official majority was maintained by the addition of two official members. McCallum had pointed out that the best representatives of the masses were the Government Agents and the Civil Servants and not the English educated middle class, but no Government Agent of the backward areas was included in the Council. The nominated Sinhalese and Tamil members had hitherto belonged to the Goigama and the Vellāla communities respectively. In the new Council the second Sinhalese and Tamil seats were given to members of the Karāva community, which in the Sinhalese districts had grown in wealth and influence. The Educated Ceylonese chose Sir Ponnambalam Ramanathan, a Tamil, as their member, and he by his exceptional services retained the seat till the next reform of the Legislative Council. Thus the Low-country Sinhalese obtained two representatives, the Kandyans one, the Indian Tamils (who formed nearly half the Tamil population) none, while the number of Ceylon Tamils in the new council equalled that of the Low-country and Kandyan Sinhalese, who in point of population were more than four times their number.[1]

On the whole the reforms helped to perpetuate the divisions in society, the special interests of which the British system of administration for over a century had tended to obliterate. Though the Educated Ceylonese electorate brought together the English-educated classes among the Sinhalese, the Tamils and the Muslims, the grant of separate electorates to the Europeans and the Burghers helped these communities to consider themselves as separate entities rather than as citizens of Ceylon.

Legislative Council of 1912
Unofficials 10

Nominated			*Elected*		
Low-country Sinhalese	..	2	Europeans	.. ..	2
Tamils	..	.. 2	Burghers	.. ..	1
Kandyans	..	.. 1	Educated Ceylonese	..	1
Muslims	..	.. 1			

Officials 11

CHAPTER X

CONSTITUTIONAL DEVELOPMENTS (1913-1948)

1. THE MANNING REFORMS

The constitutional reforms inaugurated by Sir William Manning (1918-1925) and Sir Graeme Thomson (1931-1933) were the most significant political events during the two decades subsequent to the rule of McCallum. There were undoubtedly other important changes. The development of communications continued. The railway was extended to Badulla, Trincomalee and Batticaloa, connecting all the principal towns of the island with Colombo. Motor traffic became popular, and roads were not only extended but also improved to make them suitable for cars and buses. Ceylonese began to take a more important part in planting enterprises, especially in the cultivation of rubber and coconuts. Government continued to help the agricultural industries and to encourage other industrial undertakings; and in order to give Ceylonese facilities to obtain credit on reasonable terms, a state-aided bank was established in 1938. Trade grew both within the country and with foreign countries. The repair of irrigation works was continued with vigour and the cultivation of paddy was extended. Education spread further. The pay and prospects of teachers were considerably improved and the standard of education raised. The content of vernacular education was gradually changed in order to bring it into line with modern developments. A University College was established in 1921 and was transformed into a University in 1942. The health services were rapidly extended. The Buddhist and Hindu revival made further progress and Buddhist and Hindu schools grew quickly in number and efficiency. Government services continued to expand and Ceylonese were associated in increasing numbers in the higher services. A beginning was made in 1938 to replace chief headmen by Divisional Revenue Officers. Local self-government made great strides with the establishment of Urban Councils and Village Committees. All these did not lead to any radical changes. They merely carried further a process begun earlier. But the constitutional reforms gradually weakened British control over Ceylon and enabled the Ceylonese to acquire much power in the management of their own affairs.

It has been pointed out that the reform of the Legislative Council in 1912 had not met the wishes of the Sinhalese and Tamil middle class. It had perpetuated racial representation and had failed to bring the Legislative Council into line with the developments in administration. It had neither satisfied the political aspirations of the middle class nor met the claims of Ceylonese for equality of status with the ruling race. After McCallum's time the middle class grew in strength with the extension of plantations and trade, the expansion of government services, and the growth of the medical, the legal, and the teaching professions, and by 1917 it began to ask once more for a reform of the constitution.

The agitation for reform this time received an impetus from a number of new factors. In May and June 1915, during the Great War, riots occurred in certain parts of the island when some Moors suffered at the hands of some Sinhalese. The British officials, probably owing to the war, exaggerated the gravity of these local disturbances, and as had happened in 1848 it was imagined that the unrest represented a conspiracy against British rule. Resorting to severe measures of repression under martial law, they punished and executed many innocent persons. Some of these acts of repression were condemned even by the British Governor, Sir John Anderson (1916-1918), the successor of Sir Robert Chalmers (1913-1916) in whose time the riots occurred, and they roused a considerable amount of hostile feeling against the British. The Sinhalese in particular realized that the only way they could prevent the repetition of such acts of misrule was by obtaining some control over the administration.

The agitation for constitutional reforms in India did not cease after the establishment of the Morley-Minto Councils in 1909, and towards the end of 1916 the Indian National Congress and the Muslim League asked for a considerable advance in self-government. The British Government in Britain and in India could not ignore this united request. Besides they had to recognize the services rendered by India during the War. Further they had declared that they were fighting to defend the cause of national freedom and democracy and had championed the ideals of self-development and self-determination for national units.

Up to this time the British had not thought it possible to grant parliamentary institutions to a country like India whose peoples were not homogeneous. But now they began to look upon the Indian problem from a fresh angle and in August 1917 Edward

Montagu, the Secretary of State for India, made an important pronouncement which included the following statement: 'The policy of His Majesty's Government, with which the Government of India are in complete accord, is that of the increasing association of Indians in every branch of the administration and *the gradual development of self-governing institutions with a view to the progressive realization of responsible government in India as an integral part of the British Empire*'.

Montagu did not stop at this definition of the goal of British policy in India and the method of attaining it, which repudiated all previous British declarations of India's unfitness for parliamentary institutions. He visited India at the close of the year, and in 1918 with Lord Chelmsford, the Viceroy, issued the joint *Report on Indian Constitutional Reforms.* The following year an Act of Parliament granted representative government at the Centre and a small measure of self-government to the provinces of India. The new Legislative Assembly consisted of 145 members, of whom 52 were elected by general electorates and 52 by special electorates. The rest consisted of 26 officials and 15 non-official nominated members. The Council of State, the upper chamber, consisted of 60 members of whom 34 were elected. The Viceroy's Executive Council consisted of 7 members, 3 of whom were Indians. Executive responsibility in the provinces was vested partly in officials and partly in elected representatives of the Provincial Councils, and thus was set up the system called dyarchy.

The British Empire at this time was viewed as consisting of two sections. One part like India and Ceylon was held in trust and the other like the Dominions in partnership. The reforms of 1919 formed the first step in transferring India from the first group to the second. The educated classes in Ceylon naturally expected that, in accordance with the ideals proclaimed during the war and the declarations made regarding India, the British would grant the beginnings of responsible government to Ceylon too.

A third factor strengthened the movement for reform. Reference has been made to the revival of Buddhism and Hinduism as a result of the grant of religious toleration by the British. This revival created an interest in the ancient cultures not only of the Sinhalese and the Tamils but also of the Muslims and the Burghers. The Sinhalese and the Tamils now began to magnify the worth of their past civilization, which under British rule they had underrated. Th s cultural revival, while it naturally made the Burghers realize the closeness of their connection with the British, strengthened the political and economic reaction of the Sinhalese and the Tamils against British domination by drawing into the movement for reform a large number of persons from among those who had not received an education on modern lines.

The agitation for reform in Ceylon began in April, 1917 under the vigorous leadership of Sir Ponnambalam Arunāchalam. The Ceylon Reform League was formed in May, and a Public Conference was held in December to consider the nature of the reforms that should be demanded. In December, 1919 the Low-country Sinhalese, a considerable number of Tamils, and a few others representing other communities formed the Ceylon National Congress. Following the memorials sent earlier to the Secretary of State, the Congress demanded a constitution similar to that recommended by Lord Willingdon for the Presidency of Bombay. It asked for a council of about 50 members, of whom four-fifths were to be territorially elected and the rest nominated officials and unofficials. It asked further for an elected Speaker, the retention of the control of the budget, wide male franchise and restricted female franchise, as well as the inclusion of three Ceylonese in the Executive Council with portfolios, two of whom were to be chosen from the elected members of the Legislative Council. In other words the Ceylonese demanded parliamentary institutions for Ceylon : full representative government and an executive partially responsible to the legislature.

In response to these demands the Secretary of State in consultation with Governor Manning issued in August, 1920 an Order-in-Council. The new constitution granted by it was less liberal than the Montagu-Chelmsford constitution of the Central Government of India. It resembled more the type of council granted to the provinces by the Morley-Minto reforms in 1909. It perpetuated communal representation. It continued the special electorates for the Europeans and the Burghers. It dropped the Educated Ceylonese Seat which brought into one common electorate Low-country and Kandyan Sinhalese, Tamils and Muslims. It gave an additional nominated seat to the Kandyans and a nominated seat to the Indians. It gave representation to special interests. The Chamber of Commerce and the Low-country Products Association were given an elected member each, and 3 nominated seats were reserved for other special interests. The number of official seats was increased to 14, and the Sinhalese and the Tamils were given 11 members on a territorial basis. Colombo was given 1, the rest of the Western Province 2, and the remaining provinces 1 each. Even these territorial electorates were semi-communal, as all minorities other than Ceylon Tamils, were excluded from them, even Kandyans.

The reforms introduced the principle of representative government, but in reality it gave no real power to the Ceylonese. Though this Council of 37 was to contain an unofficial majority, the elected members numbered only 16. These included three Europeans who in any vital issue could be expected to support the 14 officials. Government had also little to fear from the seven nominated members who normally would support the power to which they owed their seats. Thus Government had a good chance of commanding a majority in the Council.[1]

Later Government included three non-officials in the Executive Council. Of these only one was a member of the Legislative Council, and even he was not an elected member but one who occupied a nominated seat. This showed that there was no intention to grant even the beginnings of responsible government.

The Order-in-Council gave, as the Morley-Minto reforms did in India, further extraordinary powers to the Governor. He was allowed the right to stop the discussion of any bill or resolution, to limit the time of any discussion, and to suspend unofficial members.

The Ceylon National Congress condemned the Order-in-Council as it ' introduced invidious distinctions between communities, created special interests, and denied even the beginnings of responsible government '. The exclusion of the Kandyans from the territorial electorates was characterized as an attempt to divide the Sinhalese. Taking the view that the reforms could not be given a fair trial, the Congress decided not to participate in the new Council.

1 Legislative Council of 1921

Elected		*Nominated*	
Colombo	1	Kandyans	2
Western Province	2	Muslims	1
Other Provinces	8	Indians	1
Burghers	1	Special Interests	3
Europeans	2	Officials	14
L.C.P.A.	1		
Chamber of Commerce	1	Total	37

Manning took no serious notice of these protests and proceeded to create electorates. The Low-country Products Association which had to choose a member refused to elect one. Manning then made overtures to the Congress. He offered to a deputation of the Congress a further instalment of reforms based on the recommendations made by the new council provided the Congress co-operated. In December, 1920 the Congress accepted Manning's offer.

Sir Ponnambalam Arunāchalam and a few others did not expect anything good from participation in such a council, and their expectations were more than fulfilled. The new Legislative Council, constituted in June, 1921, consisted of 11 Low-country Sinhalese, 3 Tamils, 3 Europeans, 2 Burghers, 2 Kandyans, 1 Muslim and 1 Indian. The Ceylon Tamils broke away from the Congress soon after on the ground that Congress refused to support a reserved seat for the Tamils of the Western Province in spite of a promise made by two prominent Sinhalese Congressmen, and submitted their own demands in a separate memorial to the Secretary of State. They asked for the Tamils two-thirds of the number of Sinhalese seats on account of the importance of the Tamil community, whose representatives in the previous council were equal in number to those of the Sinhalese. The Low-country Sinhalese who now formed the main body of the Ceylon National Congress knew that the movement in India succeeded because the Muslims united with the Hindus. They tried to win back the Tamils by offering to support the allocation of far more seats for the Northern and the Eastern Provinces than their population warranted. But the Tamils appear to have been won over by Manning just as the Muslims in India were won over by Minto. Thus the demands of the Congress had little chance of being supported in a council whose members were chosen on communal lines. However necessary territorial representation was for a modern democratic state, the Tamils and the other minorities did not support demands which gave the Sinhalese a definite advantage over them.

In December, 1921 Sir James Peiris, who had taken the lead in co-operating with Government, proposed in the Legislative Council reforms on the lines demanded by the Ceylon National Congress. He asked for a council of 45 members consisting of 28 territorially elected members (of which he agreed to allot 9 to the Northern and the Eastern Provinces), 11 members for the minorities, and 6 officials. He also moved that the Council should be presided over by an elected Speaker and that the franchise qualification should be lowered. In February 1922, the Tamils, the Europeans, the Burghers, the Muslims and the Indian members of the Council submitted a joint memorandum asking for a council of 45 members consisting of 19 territorially elected members, 11 communally elected members, 3 nominated non-officials and 12 officials.

On the whole Manning objected to the proposals of the Congress representatives. Arguing as Minto did in India, that the population of Ceylon was not homogeneous, and, that the social structure was founded on a communal basis, and supporting the demand of the Tamils and the minorities that representation should be on communal lines, he opposed the grant of 28 territorially elected seats. He recommended instead a council of 47 ; and, following the proposals made by an Allocation Committee of the Council, suggested a seat each for the Ūva and the North-Central Provinces, 2 each for the Sabaragamuva, the North-Western, the Central, the Southern and the Eastern Provinces, 5 for the Northern Province, 1 for Colombo, 3 for the rest of the Western Province, 3 elected seats for the Europeans, 2 for the Burghers, and 1 for the Tamils of the Western Province, 3 nominated seats for the Muslims, 2 for the Indians and 3 for special interests, besides 12 seats for officials.

In other words he suggested 21 territorially elected seats (14 for predominantly Sinhalese areas and 7 for Tamil areas), 6 communally elected seats (3 for Europeans, 2 for Burghers and 1 for Ceylon Tamils), 5 communally nominated seats (3 for Muslims and 2 for Indians), 3 nominated seats for special interests, and 12 seats for officials. His avowed object was to make it impossible for one community to dominate the rest, but in fact he made it impossible for the Sinhalese and the Tamils who demanded the reforms to outvote the officials and the other minorities. He probably expected that in matters of vital importance Government would be able to obtain a majority with the votes of the officials, the nominated members, and the Europeans and the Burgher members.

The only important proposal of the Congress representatives to which Manning agreed was the inclusion in the territorial electorates of all those qualified to vote. This was the most far-sighted proposal as it was meant to weld together the various peoples of the island ; and it was accepted both by Manning and the supporters of communal representation who probably saw that it further reduced the power of the Sinhalese.

Manning also objected to the widening of the franchise. He refused to allow an elected Speaker but agreed to an elected Vice-President as in the Morley-Minto Councils. He refused also the inclusion of elected members in the Executive Council or the grant of portfolios to non-officials. He obviously did not wish to have in his executive members who would have to be loyal to their constituents. In other words he did not propose to grant even the beginnings of responsible government. The executive was meant to be responsible to the Governor alone and the Governor to the Secretary of State and Parliament.

The Ceylon National Congress opposed the recommendations of Manning once more, but the Secretary of State refused to make any fundamental change. He agreed with Manning that for an indefinite period representation would have to be communal, on the ground that it would take many years for the mass of the electorate to develop a political instinct strong enough to rise above racial and religious divisions. But he made a few concessions to appease the Congress. He agreed to a second seat for Colombo and a third seat for the Southern Province, thus giving two more seats to the Low-country Sinhalese, who according to the proposals ran the risk of securing less seats than in 1920. These additions increased the territorially elected members to 23 and the Sinhalese and the Tamil representatives to 24, but left them still in a minority in a council of 49. The Secretary of State also yielded to the demands of the Muslims and the Indians which were supported by the Congress representatives, and agreed to the election of Muslim and Indian members. Thus he increased the elected Ceylonese members to 29, and so not only gave Ceylon representative government as the Montagu-Chelmsford reforms had given to India, but also upset the delicately balanced structure of representation proposed by Manning which might have enabled the successful working of the reforms.

Though the reforms finally granted in Ceylon resembled in many respects the Montagu-Chelmsford reforms in relation to the Central Government, the position taken by the Montagu-Chelmsford Report differed in two important respects. The Report once more declared faith in the principles of liberalism. It took the view that liberty alone made people fit for the exercise of it. It rejected the view hitherto held that India would have to wait for *swaraj* till its population bacame homogeneous, and not only promised India self-government by successive stages but also proposed the grant of a first instalment.

The Report further objected to communal electorates. It refused to accept that communal representation was an inevitable stage in the development of a non-political people. 'Divisions by creeds and classes', it declared, 'means the creation of political camps organized against each other, and teaches men to think as partisans and not as citizens; and it is difficult to see how the change from this system to national representation is ever to occur. The British Government is often accused of dividing men in order to govern them. But if it unnecessarily divides them at the very moment when it proposes to start them on the road to governing themselves, it will find it difficult to meet the charge of being hypocritical or short-sighted'

Why did not the Secretary of State and Manning make a similar pronouncement regarding the future of Ceylon, promising self-government by successive stages? Why did they not help to strengthen Ceylon's growing sense of nationalism by giving it a constitution which would have welded together the various communities, instead of opening themselves to the charge of being hypocritical or short-sighted by strengthening communalism through the constitution they granted? It is true that insuperable difficulties made the authors of the Report agree to continue the separate electorates established by Minto; and that the Act of 1919 gave separate electorates not only to the Muslims but also to the other minorities. But was there a justification for increasing separate electorates in Ceylon, where racial, religious and caste distinctions were far less deep-rooted, and the welding of the interests of the various communities had been more effectively carried out than in India?

The probable explanation is that the Imperial Government had as yet no clear policy of how it was going to treat in the future that section of the Empire which it held in trust. The importance of Ceylon owing to its strategic position in relation to India and British communications with the East was fully realized at this time as a result of the war, and this may have deterred the consideration of any proposal to start the people of Ceylon on the road to self-government. The Order-in-Council of 1920 shows that as in 1911 the Imperial Government did not mean to treat the Legislative Council of Ceylon as more than a means of learning how the measures of Government were likely to affect the people in order to prevent any discontent turning into disaffection. Since it had to make some political concessions, it probably decided to give

Ceylon a legislature like the Morley-Minto provincial councils based on communal divisions. These were never considered by their authors as a step towards parliamentary government. When this measure of reform was rejected by the two largest communities, the Imperial Government appears to have extended communal representation further and placed the Sinhalese and the Tamils in a minority, hoping by this means to carry on British rule with undiminished power for a further indefinite period. After all, the process of unification was never intended to weaken the power the British held over Ceylon. When British rule was challenged as a result of it, Government probably did not mind reversing its past policy in order to maintain its power.

2. THE DONOUGHMORE CONSTITUTION

The Manning Reforms of 1920 might have had a chance of success ; but the const tution of 1924, especially in the form modified by the Secretary of State, could not function successfully. The Montagu-Chelmsford Report pointed out in 1918 that the Morley-Minto provincial legislative councils (none of which had an elected Indian unofficial majority) made it difficult for the executive to discharge its functions efficiently. What chance was there for the executive in Ceylon to carry out its measures through a council with a Ceylonese elected unofficial majority and with powers of financial control which the Indian councils never had ?

Manning was certainly correct when he declared that social divisions in Ceylon were communal. There was little or no intermarriage between the various races and castes and they formed more or less separate entities. In recent times racial cleavages had been accentuated further owing to the cultural revival. Besides the various communities had not all attained to the same stage of development at the time of the British occupation, and little had been done since then to develop and educate the more backward, with the result that only those communities who were at an advantage owing to their social or economic position were able to turn to good account the new opportunities afforded by Government. The Kandyans and the Muslims suffered chiefly because they had not the same opportunity for education as the Low-country Sinhalese and the Tamils. The Tamils living in the Dry Zone could not benefit directly by the great economic change that resulted from the establishment of the plantations, and depended on employment in the government services for their advancement. At this time openings for employment outside Ceylon in Further India began to be closed to them, and in face of the competition from the Low-country Sinhalese they naturally began to be alarmed about their future. Therefore the Muslims and the Kandyans began to develop a greater sense of group solidarity in order to struggle for a share in the place and power secured by the more advanced communities, while the Tamils and the Burghers did likewise to retain the position they had already attained. During the reform debate, which was really a scramble for power, the Tamils and the minorities usually combined against the Sinhalese; and when the Sinhalese and the Tamils united, the minorities joined hands with the officials against them.

But Manning ignored the fact that the British, though not deliberately, had welded the interests of the various communities to such an extent as to prevent them from dividing on communal lines once the reforms were granted. In 1815 with the conquest of the Kandyan Kingdom, Ceylon had been politically united and the British had steadily followed a policy of centralization and unification. As a result of Colebrooke's recommendations the areas occupied by the Low-country Sinhalese in the west and the south, by the Tamils in the north and the east, and by the Kandyans in the central parts had been brought under a common administrative system, and Ceylon had been divided into five provinces regardless of all communal divisions. At the same time on Cameron's proposal Ceylon had been provided with a common system of law courts, and all persons Europeans and Ceylonese, irrespective of race and caste, had been accorded equal rights in the sight of the law.

This political and administrative unification had been followed by an economic unification. The British Government by abolishing *rājakāriya* and trade monopolies rendered possible the mobility of labour and the development of private trade. Further it had encouraged the development of plantations, the products of which were for trade and not for local consumption. These things had tended to weld together the interests of the people of different districts, whereas under the old agrarian economy they lived more or less in isolation indifferent to what was happening in the other parts of the island.

This economic unification had been further strengthened by the construction of roads, the railway, the telegraph and the telephone. These in turn had enabled the development of the postal system, and all of them had brought the various parts of the island into closer contact. They had also helped the Central Government to extend its control over the provinces and developed a unified form of government for the whole island.

Moreover the spread of English had knit together the educated classes of the various communities. It had given them a common medium of speech and to some extent a common outlook, and had enabled them to come together socially. In short as a result of this process of unification the factors making for unity in Ceylon were stronger than those that divided the people.

The new councils brought the middle class into power. It had carried on the agitation for reform to obtain power for itself, and now it commanded a majority in the Council. Normally it ceased to divide on communal lines, and gave little opportunity to the executive to carry out its measures as it wished, or the Governor to discharge to his satisfaction his responsibilities to the Secretary of State.

Sir Hugh Clifford (1925-1927), wno succeeded Manning, reported to the Secretary of State that the new constitution did not work satisfactorily, and a Commission consisting of the Earl of Donoughmore (Chairman), Sir Matthew Nathan, Sir Geofirey Butler and Dr. Drummond Shiels, who were representative of the Conservative, the Liberal and the Labour parties in Parliament, was appointed 'to visit Ceylon and report on the working of the existing constitution and on any difficulties of administration which may have arisen in connection with it; to consider any proposals for the revision of the Constitution that may be put forward, and to report what, if any, amendments of the Order-in-Council now in force should be made'. The Commission arrived in Ceylon in November 1927, made their investigations and returned to England in February 1928, and submitted their report in June the same year.

The Commissioners found that the defects of the Ceylon constitution were the failings of merely 'representative government'. Earlier the system of government was such that the Executive was all-powerful and was in no way bound to accede to the wishes of the Legislature. The reforms had transferred the power to a Legislature which did not have the power to take the place of the government it opposed. The Legislature had no power to enforce its decisions. Nor had the Executive the power to act as it could not command a majority in the Legislative Council.

The Executive had not sufficient control over finance. It alone could initiate expenditure, but the control of finance was in the hands of the unofficials. In India the Morley-Minto Provincial Councils were given no such financial powers; but in Ceylon when the unofficial majority was established, the control of the budget granted to the Legislative Council in 1867 was not withdrawn. Hence the Finance Committee, which consisted mainly of unofficials, began to exercise more power than the Executive Council.

The constitution emphasized the distinction between official and elected members. Two elected members were included in the Executive Council which consisted of five officials and four unofficials, but only after they had severed their connection with the electorate and become nominated members. Thus the Executive Council with the official majority had no link with the unofficial elected majority in the Legislative Council. These conditions made a breach between the Executive and the Legislature inevitable. The unofficials drifted into a permanent opposition, and, as they were never expected to take up the responsibility for governing the country, they launched irresponsible attacks on the actions of the Executive.

The Government could have carried out its measures with the official vote alone by exercising the special powers granted to it by the constitution. As such action would have nullified the Legislature, it tried to win the co-operation of the unofficials by giving ground, compromising, and virtually surrendering its powers. Thus it reduced itself to impotence and the Governor who alone was responsible for the administration of the island could not carry out his functions satisfactorily.

Having condemned the Manning constitution the Commissioners considered what type of constitution would suit Ceylon. The next step from representative government is responsible government, but the Commissioners could not find their way to recommend such a change. It seemed to them that the Ceylonese had yet to acquire a practical training in the art of government. They did not possess a sufficient corporate spirit as their patriotism was more racial than national. The minorities were opposed to the grant of full responsible government. So the Commissioners proposed the grant to Ceylonese of a fair share of responsibility for their government.

Once they decided to place Ceylon on the road to self-government, they considered three other problems. The Tamils and the other minorities demanded the continuance of communal representation, but the Commissioners took the same stand with regard to it as the Montagu-Chelmsford Report. 'We have unhesitatingly come to the conclusion', they declared 'that communal representation is, as it were, a canker on the body politic, eating deeper and deeper into the vital energies of the people, breeding self-interest, suspicion and animosity, poisoning the new growth of political consciousness and effectively preventing the development of a national or corporate spirit. There can be no hope of binding together the diverse elements of the population, in a realization of their common kinship and an acknowledgment of common obligations to the country of which they are all citizens, as long as the system of communal representation, with all its disintegrating influences, remains a distinctive feature of the constitution'.

The Commissioners did not consider that the same need existed in Ceylon to perpetuate communal representation as in India. Most, if not all, of the communal representatives of the Legislative Council had risen above narrow sectionalism and had shown an interest in matters affecting the general welfare of the island. Further, communal electorates in Ceylon had no antiquity to justify their continuance, and its introduction had led to unfortunate results. Therefore they recommended its abolition, but, to prevent a sudden change, they recommended the establishment of 12 nominated seats for minorities of which 6 were to be given to Europeans. To allay further the fears of minorities they recommended that the Governor be given the power to refuse assent to any Bill where persons of any particular community or religion are made liable to any disabilities or restrictions to which persons of other communities or religions are not also subjected or made liable, or are granted advantages not extended to persons of other communities or religions

The Commissioners next examined the question of the franchise. In 1920 an educational and property qualification had limited it more or less to the middle class. Manning had objected to its extension in 1924, and the electorate consisted of only 204,997 persons or 4 per cent. of the population. The Commissioners noticed the backwardness of social and industrial legislation and the primitive character of the provincial government which compared unfavourably with the comparatively advanced system of government in the towns. They therefore concluded that before any further responsibility was granted to Ceylonese to manage their own affairs Government had to be made fully representative of the mass of the people. After considering many proposals they recommended the enfranchisement of men over twenty-one and of women over thirty.

Lastly they inquired into the position of government servants. There were charges of unfair criticism of heads of departments and officials by legislative councillors. After examining these, they proposed that all matters affecting the salary and emoluments, pensions and gratuities of all government services be left to the decision of the Secretary of State, and the appointments to the Governor. They also recommended the appointment of a Public Services Commission to advise the Governor regarding appointments, promotion, and other matters connected with the services.

Finally they suggested a novel expedient for the solution of Ceylon's constitutional problem. They did not consider a parliamentary form of government suitable for Ceylon as there was no party system and divisions were possible only on communal lines. As the members of the Legislative Council displayed a predominating interest in administration, they thought it would be inexpedient, if not impracticable, to exclude from the provinces of the Council the executive business of Government. They proposed therefore the establishment for the government of this country a system which had so far worked satisfactorily in the somewhat different sphere of international government. They recommended the establishment of a State Council which would give both responsibility and power to its members. It was to possess legislative powers as a general body. It was also to exercise executive powers. The departments of government were to be divided into ten groups. Three of them were to be in charge of officers of state, the Chief Secretary, the Financial Secretary and the Attorney-General (now the Legal Secretary), who were to be members of the State Council but without the right to vote. The remaining seven groups were to be controlled by the elected members of the State Council who were to be divided into seven executive committees of Home Affairs, Agriculture and Lands, Local Administration, Health, Labour, Industry and Commerce, Education, and Communications and Works. These committees were to elect their chairmen, and these chairmen along with the officers of state were to form the

Board of Ministers. The State Council was to consist of 65 territorially elected members, in addition to the twelve nominated members. Officials, of course, had no place in such a council where there was no question of commanding a majority.

The proposals of the Donoughmore Commission were at first strongly opposed by the Legislative Council, and Sir Herbert Stanley (1927-1931) who succeeded Clifford, submitted in June 1929 to the Secretary of State his own observations on the Report and the criticisms of it by the Legislative Council.

Stanley did not agree with the Commissioners on a number of minor matters. He did not think that the constitution of 1924 was an unqualified failure, but that Government in collaboration with the unofficials had achieved much. He admitted that the Executive Council had to be less absolute than before, but he did not agree that all important business was diverted from it to the Finance Committee. He supported the view that the attitude of the unofficials led to a sense of uneasiness and insecurity among the senior officers of the government service, but at the same time he pointed out that no class of government servants had suffered any loss of pay or of leave or pension rights through any action of the Council. Thus he considered that some of the conclusions of the Commissioners were too sweeping in their condemnation of the Manning constitution and its working, but he fully supported their main proposals and defended them against the objections raised by the Legislative Council.

The Legislative Council, whose representation was based on communal lines, naturally objected to the abolition of communal representation. The Sinhalese supported the Commissioners as its abolition coincided with their interests and would give them a preponderant position in the new council. On the other hand the Ceylon Tamils objected to the establishment of electorates based on numbers which would diminish their political influence. They feared that if this happened their prospects of employment in government service too would suffer. The Muslims and the Burghers too supported communal representation as it was their only safeguard against the risk of political submersion. Stanley sympathized with the fears of the Tamils, the Muslims, and the Burghers, but agreed with the Commissioners that any advance towards self-government should be accompanied by the abolition of communal representation. Even if it were perpetuated he did not think voting in the Council would follow communal lines. Besides it was not a desirable ingredient in the composition of a democratic institution.

The question of franchise too led to much controversy. In one respect the Legislative Council went further than the Commissioners and suggested the grant of the vote to all over 21, including women. But a large section, especially the Sinhalese members, objected to the grant of manhood suffrage to a floating population like that of the Indian labourers on the estates. Stanley agreed with the Commissioners on the necessity of broadening the electoral basis if there was to be an advance towards self-government. But he did not support the view expressed by some Indians that the proposal for the restriction of the franchise was actuated by prejudice against Indian labourers as Indians. He agreed with the Commissioners that 'the privilege of voting should be confined to those who have an abiding interest in the country or who may be regarded as permanently settled in the island'.

The other features which were strongly opposed were the system of Executive Committees and the wide powers given to the Governor. The Executive Committee system was condemned 'either as unworkable or as likely to cause undue delay in the transaction of business, or as derogatory to the status and incompatible with the proper functions of a Minister, or as embarrassing to Heads of Departments in the discharge of their duties and in their relations, with Ministers, or as conducive to the substitution of compromises and bargains for a clearly defined policy, or as unjustifiably expensive, or as a check upon the development of a full sense of responsibility, or as an impediment to further constitutional evolution towards the desired goal'. Stanley considered the Executive Committee system fundamental to the whole scheme of government proposed in the Report, and objected to any change as it would destroy the balance of the scheme. He objected also to any reduction of the powers recommended to be granted to the governor in view of the important changes proposed and the wide powers that would be granted to the Council. The Legislative Council also objected to any abridgement of the financial and other powers and privileges which it had hitherto enjoyed. The reference was mainly to the powers they exercised over the salaries and other emoluments of the public servants. Stanley considered the arrangement proposed by the Commissioners necessary during a period of transition.

The Secretary of State agreed on the whole with Stanley. He approved of the abolition of communal representation, the establishment of the Executive Committee system, and the grant of additional powers to the Governor. He agreed to the grant of the vote to every man and woman over 21, and accepted Stanley's proposal that domicile should be the test for the inclusion of the name of a person in the Register. But contrary to Stanley's views he agreed to the proposal of the Legislative Council to have a council of 50 territorially elected members, and eight nominated members of whom four were to be Europeans. The proposals of the Secretary of State were strongly opposed in the Legislative Council, but they were finally accepted by the unofficials by 19 votes against 17.

The Donoughmore Constitution was established by Sir Graeme Thomson in 1931. A Board of Ministers consisting of seven Ceylonese ministers, three of whom belonged to the minority communities, replaced the Executive Council which came into existence with the establishment of the Crown Colony system of government in 1802. Sir Baron Jayatilaka, who had played an important part in the movement for reform, became the Leader of the House and the Vice-Chairman of the Board of Ministers. One of the objections raised against the Donoughmore Constitution was that it did not grant full responsible government, and the Tamils of the Jaffna Peninsula, influenced by the younger people, refused to participate for some time in a constitution which fell far short of national demands.

3. THE SOULBURY REFORMS AND THE ATTAINMENT OF INDEPENDENCE

Apart from this the Constitution itself did not satisfy two sections of the members of the State Council. One disapproved of the Committee system and the reduction of financial power. The other objected to it because of the abolition of communal representation. Requests for changes were made from 1932, but the Secretary of State refused to consider any radical alteration of the Constitution before it was given a fair trial. The Donoughmore Constitution, however, was meant as a preliminary to the grant of responsible government; and in 1937 Sir Andrew Caldecott who succeeded Sir Reginald Stubbs (1933-1937) was requested by the Secretary of State to examine the constitutional position and submit his recommendations.

In November 1938, Sir Andrew submitted his recommendations to the Secretary of State. He objected to the proposals to restrict the franchise or curtail the powers of the Governor. There was once more the demand for a return to communal representation by the reservation of fifty or forty per cent. of the seats to the Tamils and the minorities. Sir Andrew refused to make any concession to such demands as it would 'perpetuate sectionalism, and preclude the emergence of true political parties on true political issues'. But he thought that electoral areas might be rearranged so that minority communities might secure more seats. He agreed with the objections that had been raised against the system of Executive Committees, and suggested their abolition as 'there is no determining, co-ordinating, eliminating, controlling, or designing force behind the administrative machine; everything depends upon bargaining and compromise. As a result there can be no fixation and concentration either of policy or responsibility'. If they were to be retained, he recommended that appointments to government services should not be referred to them, but to an independent Public Services Commission. He was for the establishment of a cabinet system of government by the exclusion of the officers of state, and the appointment of two other ministers to be entrusted with their work.

The reform proposals were debated in the State Council and they led to no general agreement. Therefore the Secretary of State felt that the matter should be re-examined after the war was over. The war had the effect of making the British once more emphasize their ideals of freedom and democracy and offer Dominion Status to India. In 1942 the State Council asked for Dominion Status for Ceylon. The Secretary of State in reply promised the fullest possible development of self-governing institutions, and in 1943 made the following declaration: 'The post-war re-examination of the reform of Ceylon's constitution, to which His Majesty's Government stands pledged, will be directed towards the grant to Ceylon by Order of His Majesty in Council of full responsible government under the Crown in all matters of internal civil administration Further, if the Ministers formulated a constitution on these lines, which would receive the approval of three-fourths of the members of the State Council, the Secretary of State agreed to examine it by means of a Commission or Conference.

Accordingly, in 1944, the Ministers submitted a draft constitution to the Secretary of State and pressed for its examination immediately. They recommended a unicameral legislature of ninety-five elected and six nominated members and left it to the new Council to establish a second chamber, if it so desired. They did not yield to the demands made at the time to restrict the franchise or to restore communal electorates. But they gave the minorities a better chance of securing a larger number of seats by providing for smaller electorates and by taking into account, in forming them, both area as well as population. By this means the North-Central, Ūva, Northern and Eastern Provinces were in a position to obtain more seats than their numbers warranted. The Ministers also provided six nominated members and in addition gave legal protection to minorities. And to allay their fears further they provided for a Public Services Commission and a Judicial Services Commission to deal with problems connected with the public and judicial services. The most important change they recommended, however was the substitution of the cabinet form of government in place of the Executive Committee system.

On July 5, 1944, the Imperial Government appointed a Commission, consisting of Lord Soulbury, a Conservative and former member of the British Cabinet, Professor J. F. Rees, a Liberal and Vice-Chancellor of the University of Wales, and F. J. Burrows a Socialist and Trade Union Leader, 'to visit Ceylon in order to examine and discuss any proposals for constitutional reforms in the Island which have the object of giving effect to the Declaration of His Majesty's Government on that subject dated 26th May, 1943; and after consultation with various interests in the Island, including minority communities, concerned with the subject of constitutional reform, to advise His Majesty's Government on all measures necessary to attain this object'

The Ministers objected to the Commission on the ground that these terms of reference was a violation of the Declaration of 1943. The Imperial Government refused to make any change and justified their action declaring that it had to be read along with the statement of 1941. The Ministers, thereupon, withdrew their Scheme and decided not to give evidence before the Commission. Their Constitution, with an explanatory memorandum, however, was published as a Sessional Paper in September 1944.

The Commission held its first meeting in London on November 30, 1944. Having examined the basic documents and discussed matters informally with the Colonial Office and the Treasury they left England on 19th December by air and arrived in Colombo on

22nd December. They examined numerous memoranda submitted to them, held public sessions, and visited almost all parts of the Island. They returned leaving Ceylon on April 7 1945 and submitted their report on July 9, 1945.

The Commission, on the whole supported the Ministers' Scheme. The modifications they made were not of a substantial nature. They refused to restrict the franchise, but recommended the establishment of a Second Chamber giving it even less powers than the House of Lords in Britain. They refused also to restore communal electorates but suggested the delimitation of electorates so as to help minorities to secure more seats.

In the meantime the State Council had demanded Dominion Status for Ceylon, and Mr. D. S. Senanayake, when he was invited for consultation by the Secretary of State, in order to secure Dominion Status demanded further modifications of the recommendations of the Soulbury Commission. The circumstances of the time were in his favour. Colonies were considered one of the chief causes of war and international opinion was tending in the direction of placing all colonies under a world organization. Though the Conference held at San Francisco did not go so far, the colonial powers that met there agreed to help the people of their colonies to attain self-government as early as possible. But the British Government which had not granted Dominion Status even to India was reluctant to make such a concession. Nevertheless the Order-in-Council of May 15, 1946 conferred on Ceylon a constitution with a higher degree of autonomy than any Dominion legally possessed before 1930. It not only gave full responsible government in all matters of internal civil administration but also some control over defence and external affairs.

But when India and Burma attained independence Mr. Senanayake persisted in his demand for similar treatment for Ceylon, and on June 18, 1947 the Secretary of State for Colonies announced that Ceylon would be granted full responsible government shortly after the new constitution came into being, and this decision was implemented on February 4, 1948. Thus ended British rule over Ceylon, but like Burma Ceylon did not sever connections with Britain altogether. Instead like India it decided to remain within the Commonwealth of Nations of which Britain was the predominant partner.

BIBLIOGRAPHY

Governors' Addresses to the Legislative Council, 1833-1903. 4 vols. Colombo.

Administration of the Affairs of Ceylon, 1896-1903. Colombo.

Progress of the Colony of Ceylon, 1904-1907. Colombo.

Review of the Administration of Ceylon, 1907-1913. Colombo.

Constitutional Documents of Ceylon, 1908-1924.

Ceylon: Report of the Special Commission on the Constitution London, 1928.

Ceylon: Report of the Commission on Constitutional Reform, London, 1945.

L. E. Blaze: *History of Ceylon.* Christian Literature Society.

S. G. Perera: *A History of Ceylon for Schools.* Associated Newspapers of Ceylon, Ltd.

L. A. Mills: *Ceylon under British Rule.* Oxford.

C. R. de Silva: *Ceylon under the British Occupation* (1795-1933). The Colombo Apothecaries' Co., Ltd.

P. M. Bingham: *History of the Public Works Department, Ceylon*, Colombo.

G. F. Perera: *The Ceylon Railway.* Colombo.

R. L. Brohier: *Ancient Irrigation Works of Ceylon*, Colombo. *Land, Maps and Surveys.* Colombo.

Sir Ivor Jennings: *The Constitution of Ceylon* (Second Edition). Oxford University Press.

S. Namasivayam: *The Legislatures of Ceylon.* Faber and Faber Ltd.

Robert Knox: *An Historical Relation of Ceylon.*

James Cordiner: *Description of Ceylon.*

Thomas Skinner: *Fifty Years in Ceylon.*

James Steuart: *Notes on Ceylon.*

W. H. Gregory: *An Autobiography.*

W. Digby: *Life of Morgan.*

A. C. Seneviratne: *Memoirs and Desultory Writings of the late James D' Alwis.* Colombo.

B. R. Blaze: *The Life of Lorenz.* The Associated Newspapers of Ceylon, Ltd.

W. T. KEBLE AND DEVAR SURYA SENA : *The Life of James Peiris.* Colombo.

E. R. SARATCHANDRA : *The Sinhalese Novel.* M. D. Gunasena & Co., Colombo.

H. A. WYNDHAM : *Native Education.*

H. H. DODWELL : *India.* Arrowsmith.

L. S. S. O'MALLEY : *Modern India and the West.* Oxford.

R. COUPLAND : *The Indian Problem.* Oxford.

INDEX